DR. ASHLEY N. ROBERTSON

Foreword by Dr. Gwendolyn Boyd

Mary McLeod Bethune

— *in* F L O R I D A —

Bringing Social Justice to the Sunshine State

Caitlin,
Thanks for your
support! I pray
this book inspires
you.

THE
History
PRESS

Published by The History Press
Charleston, SC 29403
www.historypress.net

Copyright © 2015 by Dr. Ashley N. Robertson
All rights reserved

First published 2015

Manufactured in the United States

ISBN 978.1.62619.983.5

Library of Congress Control Number: 2015936220

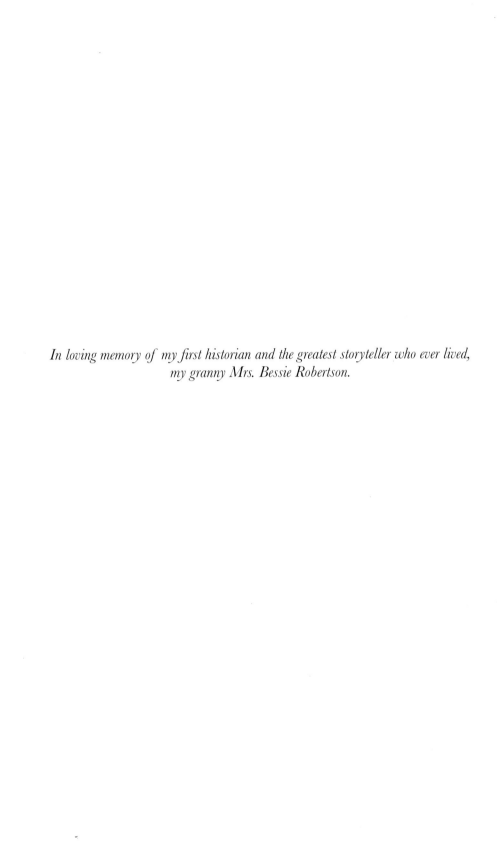

In loving memory of my first historian and the greatest storyteller who ever lived, my granny Mrs. Bessie Robertson.

Contents

Contents

Foreword

*The Delta girl is one who has been given the opportunity of
education and broad development.*

In 1923, at the fifth national convention, Mary McLeod Bethune became
an honorary member of the Delta Sigma Theta Sorority. It was in that
same year that her all-girls school in Daytona Beach, Florida, merged with
Cookman Institute to become what was later known as Bethune-Cookman
College (B-CC). Founded in 1904 as the Daytona Literary and Industrial
School for the Training of Negro Girls under Mary's visionary leadership
and dedication, with the merger she became one of the first female African
American college presidents. The year 1923 was a pivotal point for Bethune,
who was the first child born free to formerly enslaved parents. For nearly two
decades, she toiled to provide quality education in segregated Florida while
also rising through the ranks as a leader in the clubwomen's movement.
In 1924, she became president of the National Association of Colored
Women's Clubs (NACW). As president, she reinforced NACW's anti–poll
tax stance, strengthened its international relations and established its first
national headquarters in Washington, D.C.

This critical study by Dr. Ashley Robertson reveals the depth of the
leadership of Mary McLeod Bethune in the state of Florida. Many know
Florida for its beautiful sandy beaches and its tourist attractions, but few are
aware of the intense racial conditions through which Bethune navigated.
This work uncovers her use of Bethune-Cookman College as a political

space to take a stance against segregation, her fearless leadership in a male-dominated society and how she galvanized women for change in her local community. Dr. Robertson also makes readers keenly aware of Bethune's role as a premier civil rights and women's rights activist dating back to the early 1900s. As the president of Alabama State University and a past national president of Delta Sigma Theta Sorority Inc., I am surely a "daughter" of Mary McLeod Bethune in many ways. Her dynamic leadership in the clubwomen's movement and her commitment to the education of African Americans cleared a path for leaders such as myself. We stand on the shoulders of Soror Bethune.

As we move forward in such an important time in history, scholarship such as this book will be a guide for our movements. We can examine how Bethune attracted the support of influential leaders to push the agenda of educational equality so that we might work to close educational gaps in the twenty-first century. We can also learn from her successes in organizing African American women to gain suffrage and take a stance against discrimination to disrupt the overturning of critical pieces of the Voting Rights Act of 1965. There are lessons to be learned from this dynamic leader, and this work should be in the hands of all agents for change standing for justice.

Dr. Gwendolyn Boyd

Acknowledgements

For I know the plans I have for you, declares the Lord, plans to prosper you and not to harm you, plans to give you a hope and a future.
—Jeremiah 29:11

Before any words are said, I would like to give honor to Jesus Christ, my Lord and Savior, for all that He has done. I am truly blessed to see the day when someone from little Oxford, North Carolina, would receive a doctorate and write a book. It was all in His plan, and I am grateful. I am also thankful for my angel, Mrs. Bessie Robertson, who left in 2004, but her words "That girl gone be something" will always be my guide to keep marching on for excellence. Thank you, Granny, for speaking positive over my life, for being my very first historian and for passing along to me the gift of storytelling. You are missed.

I would like to thank my mother, Diane, for her continued prayers and encouragement. I will never forget when you said, "Ain't nothing holdin' you back! Not even a stop sign!" You continue to give me courage, and I appreciate you. Thanks to my daddy, John, for always being a listening ear and for being a strong writer. You laid the foundations for this. To my sister and best friend, April Joy, I thank you for always being my biggest supporter. Since sixth grade we've held each other down. Dr. Kimberly Brown, you are truly a "Queen Like Me," and I can never repay you for assisting me with the direction of this book. My siStar Princess Black, you are history in the making, and your activism is an inspiration to me.

This book would not have been possible without those in Florida who have not only become my family but have also encouraged me to write this work

Acknowledgements

and share the lift of my (s)hero. I truly thank my boss, Dr. Tasha Youmans, for her continued support and for giving me so many resources to make this happen. You are the best! Thanks to Mr. Albert McLeod Bethune Jr. for being my biggest advocate and for sharing his wealth of knowledge on the life of his "Mother Dear." Ms. Patricia Pettus and Mrs. Sandra Johnson, you will never know how much I appreciate both of you. To the faculty/staff/students of Bethune-Cookman University and the Bethune Foundation, I appreciate you all for giving me the opportunity to fulfill my mission as a historian.

While writing this book there were people who went out of their way to provide me with archival materials and valuable insight, and without them this book would not have the depth that it has. Thanks to Dr. Anthony Dixon (John G. Riley Museum), Aisha Johnson (University of North Florida) and my dear friends John Fowler and Joy Kinard at the Mary McLeod Bethune Council House. Dr. Ida Jones, thanks for encouraging me to write this book and for all that you do at Moorland-Spingarn Research Center. I was given the opportunity to interview people who knew Mrs. Bethune, and I am grateful to Ms. Locklear, Mr. Lucas, Mr. Bethune and Dr. Higgins for sharing their personal stories about what Mrs. Bethune meant to them. I pray that God continues to bless you all with excellent health and memory. Special thanks also to my mentors and pioneers in the field of history and African American studies Dr. Elizabeth Clark-Lewis and Dr. Valethia Watkins.

I know that I'm going to forget someone, but know that I love you all. I want to thank Aunt Mary; Aunt Carolyn; Uncle Pete; Uncle Lee; Uncle Larry; Cousin Faye; Cousin Cassandra; Cousin Marie; Cousin Whitney Marie; Cousin Brent; God babies Destiny and DeAndre; Cousin Brandon; Cousin Derek Lalisco; God mommy Rosa; and God sisters Jessica, Latonya and Felicia for keeping me grounded. Family, I love you. My sisters Nerissa, Cliffordette, Gala, Kendra, Ava, Donna, Tiara, Tiffany, Amanee, Jerilyn, Cletra, Jessica, Shatira, Carla, Ronda, Cousin Tanya and Stacey, you all are the best friends a girl could have. To my spiritual family, Uncle Bishop, Aunt Daisy, Pastor Natashia, Pastor Dawson, First Lady Robinson and Bishop Robinson, I thank you for all of your prayers and prophetic words you've spoken into my life.

Last but not least, I would like to thank Dr. Gwendolyn Boyd for her contribution to this book. You have demonstrated true leadership as national president of Delta Sigma Theta and now as president of Alabama State University, and you are the modern-day Dr. Mary McLeod Bethune. I pray that God continues to guide you to greatness.

To everyone who picks up this book, thanks for being a "Bethune Believer" and for taking the opportunity to learn more about a woman who has changed the course of history. Please join me in building on the foundations she laid for us all.

Introduction

Although today Florida is known mostly for its tourism, when Mary McLeod Bethune arrived in Daytona Beach in 1904, she found a segregated, rural town in which African Americans were relegated to small areas. After teaching in various places, including South Carolina and Georgia, Mary McLeod Bethune made her way to Daytona Beach in September 1904 with $1.50 in her pocket, looking to start a school. On October 3, 1904, she opened the Daytona Literary and Industrial School for the Training of Negro Girls in a growing small town. As railroads were being built across the state, people moved to Florida for new opportunities, and Bethune was one of those people. Arriving with very little, she created a vital space for the African American community to congregate, discuss community issues and spark activism. Nearly 111 years later, what is known today as Bethune-Cookman University stands on the shoulders of a woman who not only shaped the political climate of Daytona but also contributed greatly to activism in Florida.

Born to formally enslaved parents, Bethune valued education and hard work from an early age. She once said, "The whole world opened to me when I learned to read." Before she was able to attend school, she worked in the cotton fields with her family and watched her mother work for nearby whites. Once, while picking up laundry with her mother, she encountered something that changed her life. She picked up a book and looked through it but was interrupted by a child who took it away and told her that she couldn't read because she was a Negro. This was a turning point; from that point on, she understood that there was something in that book she needed to know. Throughout her years, she recounted the moment and remembered it just as she did the day it happened.

Around the age of ten, she was able to formally enter school at the Trinity Presbyterian Mission School in Mayesville, South Carolina. Attending school was a dream come true, and she excelled. As she learned, she shared the knowledge with the community and her family by teaching others to read and helping local farmers calculate their wages. Before she was able to decide what to do with her life, she started with educating others, and ultimately her love for teaching would guide her. She later attended Scotia Seminary and Moody Bible College with the idea to become a missionary. She was disappointed when she was told no but not deterred. Again, she took a disappointment, which could have been a setback, and turned it into determination.

It seemed that her life began to change overnight, and in 1898, she married Albertus Bethune and became a mother just nine months later. She soon met Reverend C.J. Uggans, a pastor of a Presbyterian church in Palatka, Florida, and he encouraged her to relocate to assist with a new mission school. Having remembered being a young student of the Presbyterian school in her hometown, she felt a strong connection to the work of the church. For almost five years, she taught at the Palatka Mission School while also selling insurance for the Afro Life Insurance Company to keep her family afloat. Within the last decade, she had lived in Chicago, Savannah, Palatka, Mayesville, Augusta and Sumter, but in 1904, she moved to Daytona Beach, Florida, and until her passing in 1955, this was the place she called home.

Mary McLeod Bethune's 1904 move was the start of a new journey, and she dedicated herself to creating a better life for those around her in her local community and throughout the state. She involved herself as an educator, a political activist and a clubwoman. There was no task that involved creating change for the better in which she did not involve herself. She made use of her gift as an educator by founding a school, she used her talent for organizing to rally voters for change and she later used her influence to create a safe space for black Daytona. Her life was one of self-sacrifice and dedication.

Over the years, Bethune became an international civil rights activist, loved by many, and this book examines how her work in Florida provided a critical foundation for her influential role as a leader throughout the world. It is in Florida that she entered a racially divided town where the Ku Klux

Mary McLeod Bethune's 1943 portrait. *Courtesy of the Bethune-Cookman University Archives.*

Klan's presence was strong and built a school while standing firm against segregation. It was in the Sunshine State—with its beautiful beaches that mostly barred African Americans—that Bethune purchased a beach and created opportunity for those who might not otherwise have seen the beauty of the coastline. After creating an institution with $1.50, five little girls and faith in God—one that continues to flourish today with over

A portrait of Mary McLeod Bethune. *Courtesy of the Bethune-Cookman University Archives.*

3,700 students—it is no wonder that she would advise presidents and serve as an ambassador for the United States government. Florida was the place where Bethune committed herself to a life of activism, and today she is still honored and remembered, not only as the "First Lady of Negro America," but also as a transformative leader who had a great impact on the course of Florida's history.

$1.50, Faith in God and Five Little Girls

The Founding of Bethune-Cookman University

Mary McLeod Bethune was born to Patsy and Samuel McLeod on July 10, 1875, near rural Mayesville, South Carolina. She was the fifteenth of seventeen children and the first to be born into freedom. As she was the first of her parents' children born free, there were a lot of expectations for her life. Freedom had been a dream, and her life held unique promise because of it. When opportunities to further her education came along, young Mary did not pass them up. She attended Scotia Seminary in Concord, North Carolina (graduated in 1894), and thereafter Moody Bible Institute in Chicago, Illinois (graduated in 1895). It was after Moody that she attempted to go to Africa as a missionary, but the Presbyterian Mission Board explained to her that it was no longer allowing black missionaries to go to Africa. Although her dreams were temporarily crushed, she decided to become a teacher. Lucy Craft Laney, an educator who had opened her own school in Augusta, Georgia, offered her a position as a teacher at the Haines Normal and Industrial School. Haines was the first school for African Americans in Augusta, and it was there during her short tenure (1896–97) that Bethune adopted the idea of starting her own school and received valuable mentorship from Ms. Laney. Like Bethune, Laney was born free to formerly enslaved parents. The following year, while teaching at Kendall Institute in Sumter, South Carolina, Mary McLeod met and married a young teacher named Albertus Bethune. Nine months later, on February 3, 1899, the pair became parents when Albert McLeod Bethune was born.

Albert McLeod Bethune Sr. as a child. *Courtesy of the Bethune-Cookman University Archives.*

After living for a while in Savannah, Georgia, the family moved to Palatka, Florida, where Bethune started a small mission school at the urging of a native Presbyterian minister. After almost five years in Palatka, she was encouraged to move to Daytona since there were several African Americans moving to Daytona Beach to work on the railroads. This meant there would also be children moving, and they would be in need of an education. In September 1904, Bethune arrived in Daytona Beach with her son; her husband stayed behind in Palatka to conduct business. With $1.50 in cash, she looked for a place to rent and was able to convince the owner of a four-bedroom home to let her rent it for $11.00 a month, although she did not have all of the rent up front. On October 3, 1904, she utilized the home to officially open the Daytona Literary and Industrial School for Training Negro Girls with her son and five little girls: Lena, Lucille and Ruth Warren; Anna Geiger; and Celest Jackson.

At the time that Bethune arrived, Daytona Beach was a very progressive area. It was established in 1876, and blacks represented about half the population and had built their own stores and churches. Wealthy whites also maintained winter homes in Daytona Beach. She saw both of these populations as those that could be of assistance in starting her school. Local African Americans, including carpenters, helped build the

An early photo of students at Faith Hall, along with teaching staff and Mary Bethune, in 1920. *Courtesy of the Bethune-Cookman University Archives.*

The earliest known pictures of Mary Bethune and her all-girls school. *Courtesy of the Bethune-Cookman University Archives.*

first building—Faith Hall—while others donated dishes and food from their gardens. The black Daytona Beach community was the backbone of the school, providing much-needed encouragement. To stabilize the school and to expand her network, Bethune established an impressive board of trustees that included James N. Gamble, the wealthy co-owner of Proctor and Gamble. In the early years, she sold sweet potato pies as a way to raise funds; she also sold boiled eggs to local railroad workers for lunch. After a separation from her husband around 1907, Bethune continued to grow the school and reach out for assistance on her own. Expanding on her fundraising efforts for the school, she took her students to sing for wealthy whites who were visiting Daytona Beach on vacation and collected donations. Thomas White of White Sewing Machine Company also became a supporter of the school after seeing a performance by the school's choir. Bethune established a relationship with John D. Rockefeller, a very wealthy philanthropist and owner of Standard Oil Company, to assist with fundraising. She also enlisted the help of Booker T. Washington, founder of Tuskegee Institute, who visited her at the school in 1912. He was instrumental in helping her establish relationships with wealthy philanthropists, and she became good friends with his wife, "Lady Principal" Margaret Murray Washington. The pair later became involved in the 1920 founding of the International Council of Women of the Darker Races, an organization that was concerned with the worldwide condition of people of African descent.

Under Bethune's leadership, the school expanded and underwent several changes, particularly its name. By 1919, the school had made its third name change, transitioning from Daytona Educational and Industrial Institute to Daytona Normal and Industrial Institute. In 1923, the all-girls school began the process of merging with Cookman Institute, a coed school led by the Methodist Church. Founded in Jacksonville, Florida, in 1872, it had also been the first school to offer higher education to African Americans in the state of Florida. Although the merging of Bethune's school and Cookman Institute began in 1923, it was not until March 1925 that it became complete, and both schools collaborated to become the Daytona Cookman Collegiate Institute. Following the merger, Bethune served as president from 1923 to 1942 and from 1946 to 1947. In 1931, the school became officially known as Bethune-Cookman College. Although there were several schools founded by and for women, it was rare for African American women to serve as college presidents during Bethune's time. In fact, even Spelman College, which was founded for African American women in 1881, did not gain its first female African American president, Dr. Johnnetta Cole, until 1987. Howard University, founded in 1867, did not see its first black president, Mordecai Johnson, until 1926. For Bethune to become a college president in 1923, she was well before her time.

By 1928, the school had expanded and offered junior college and college preparatory courses; it also offered students the opportunity to gain specialized experience in its School of Commerce and School of Music, among others. The school also invested in a new Drama Department, and literary giant Zora Neale Hurston taught there for a brief time in 1934. During her tenure as president, Bethune continued to add various programs and trainings to enhance the students' skill set. She also ensured that the football team, started shortly after the merger, remained a part of the school, despite the fact that, initially, it cost the school quite a bit to maintain it. She vowed to raise the money to keep the program alive, and she did.

Digging deeper into civil rights activism, Bethune also served in advisement positions for four U.S. presidents. She served as a delegate to the Child Welfare Conference under Calvin Coolidge and worked on the National Committee on Child Welfare under the leadership of Herbert Hoover. During Franklin Delano Roosevelt's presidency, he implemented a number of programs under the New Deal, including the National Youth Administration (NYA). NYA was designed to provide work relief to students from ages sixteen to twenty-five. At the time, unemployment was at an all-time high, and the programs were

Mary Bethune dedicating the campus Log Cabin in 1939. This cabin was used for student social events. *Courtesy of the Bethune-Cookman University Archives.*

The B-CC agricultural stand where students sold harvested goods. *Courtesy of the Bethune-Cookman University Archives.*

Bethune-Cookman College, Daytona Beach, Florida academic exhibit in 1926 displaying renovated dresses made by the students.

particularly beneficial for African Americans. It also provided "student aid" to students of the same age who could no longer afford tuition. Bethune was appointed to be a representative on the advisory committee for the NYA along with Mordecai Johnson. In 1936, Roosevelt appointed her to a larger role as the head of the Office of Minority Affairs under the NYA program, making her the first black woman to head a federal agency. As the head of the division, she ensured that African Americans received their fair share of federal funding. She also ensured that African American colleges were included in the Civilian Pilot Training Program, which led to the graduation of some of the first African American pilots in the nation. The division came to an end in 1943. Under Harry Truman's administration, she served as a consultant on interracial relations and as an international delegate.

After years of success as both the founder and president of B-CC, Bethune's busy schedule took a toll on her, and in 1941, she made the decision to retire the following year. On December 15, 1942, Dr. James Colston was elected as the second president of B-CC.

Sunday Community Meetings and the Protest of Segregation

Mrs. Mary McLeod Bethune's refusal to set up a special section at her school for white folk when Mrs. Eleanor Roosevelt spoke there, was indeed a noteworthy and courageous act. By so doing she made the thirty-fifth anniversary celebration of Bethune-Cookman College, of which she is president and a founder, an epochal event, for it is unusual that a Negro in the South balks at the bidding or requests of the white folk.

During the early 1900s, when Mary McLeod Bethune came to Daytona Beach, the town was segregated, with railroad tracks as the barrier separating African Americans from the rest of the town. Less than a decade before her arrival, the landmark decision in *Plessy v. Ferguson* declared that separate but equal facilities were legal. The case brought a clear message that segregation was now the law, and throughout much of the United States, it was practiced with vigor. Midtown, the prominent center of the African American community in Daytona Beach, was filled with churches, black-owned businesses and homes. Mrs. Bethune built her school in the heart of Midtown. Over the years, she created a space for African American students and faculty/staff members to flourish through academic success, community activism and the development of young minds. Although she

Mary Bethune and Dr. James Colston in 1943 as she resigned from her presidency.
Courtesy of the Bethune-Cookman University Archives.

was able to build a safe haven, segregation permeated throughout the city even decades after she successfully established the school as a college.

Working as a photographer for the Office of War Information in 1943, Gordon Parks was sent to Daytona Beach to capture Bethune-Cookman College and Midtown. His groundbreaking photographs showed B-CC students producing farm vegetables, training in automobile mechanics and learning skills, including welding and sheet metal work, through the

Sunday Community Meetings at B-CC. *Courtesy of the Bethune-Cookman University Archives.*

Mary Bethune and First Lady Roosevelt at B-CC. *Courtesy of the Bethune-Cookman University Archives.*

National Youth Administration to support World War II efforts. While he focused largely on B-CC, Gordon took a unique look at black Daytona, particularly Midtown's Second Avenue area. He featured the Pinehaven housing projects; children of laborers; historic churches, including Stewart Memorial; and local businesses with patrons relaxing outside on the porches. For many who knew Daytona Beach as the "World's Famous Beach," it was a completely different place when you saw Parks's pictures filled with black faces and no beaches in sight. Although his work didn't comment on the fact that blacks were not allowed to go to the beach, it was clear that Midtown was their own community, completely separate from the rest of the city.

In her position as founder of Bethune-Cookman College, Bethune utilized the school as a space to protest the practices of segregation. As early as the 1920s, all races could be seen in pictures sitting together as a result of integrated seating policies during the school's Sunday Community Meetings. In a 1937 article in the *Literary Digest* about Bethune's work at B-CC, the issue of integration on the campus was discussed: "When white people come to call there are no special seats set aside for them. 'Once within the walls of the college,' says its founder, 'there are neither blacks nor whites, only ladies and gentlemen.'" Although it was illegal to hold interracial meetings, she was not intimidated by the legal system and did what she felt was right. At any given time during Sunday meetings, wealthy doctors and lawyers sat beside affluent, middle-class and poor members of the black community. Although some may have been in shock initially, eventually it became accepted that if you were going to participate in Bethune's meeting, you would do so by her rules. This simple action made her school a place of protest that went directly against the Jim Crow policies and procedures permeating America.

For those who remembered Sunday Community Meetings, they were well-attended and well-known events, and their popularity spread to the beachside tourists of Daytona Beach. Although it was rare for whites to cross into Midtown, they came to attend B-CC's Sunday afternoon event. The students, faculty and staff of the college and the local community attended and performed during the meetings. It was a time when people of all colors congregated, and all eyes were on the children of Midtown. In an interview, Mr. Harold V. Lucas Jr. fondly remembers the meetings, which he attended starting in 1939:

> *Sunday community meetings…well, first of all, you know there were not supposed to be any interracial groups meeting during this time. I remember*

community meetings from the time I was like seven or eight years old. What they would do was they would again have the concert choral type people, they would sing and we would have a program where they would talk about different things about the school. They didn't talk about issues; it was not that type of community meeting. What it was…it was a thing where white people and black people could come and enjoy music and enjoy little kids speak. And I remember the first time that I went to community meeting, and I was supposed to say my little speech and I had practiced it, you know. And I got up on the stage, and you'd stand behind the curtain; then they would open the curtain and you'd step out; and then you'd say whatever you had to say; then you'd go back behind the curtain. And when it was my time, I looked out there and said, "It's too many people." And I went back behind the curtain, and my daddy said, "No, go out there and say your speech." But the community thing was an attraction that helped to draw the people that might be interested in helping Bethune to the campus so that they could see what she was doing. And that's how Mr. Gamble and Mr. Rockefeller and Mr. White and how those people became…"Well, what is this?" They came looking for something to do. You know, they were just

Sunday Community Meetings. *Courtesy of the Bethune-Cookman University Archives.*

down here in this nice sunny weather and they didn't have anything to do on Sunday afternoons 'cause you know they didn't have TV and all of that stuff. "We'll go over there and hear those black folks sing and hear the little kids. And what's the lady's name over there that's trying to start that school?" You know they were inquiring about what was going on here because the people that she had met on the beachside were the main people that ran the community, and she convinced them. And of course you know if John D. Rockefeller was coming over here...the Proctor and Gamble man was coming over here, all his little cronies was wondering, "Well what are you going over there for?" and then they would say, "Oh man they can sing and they have little kids doing stuff and you ought to see how they are improving those grounds over there." Again improving the grounds was an element of the whole thing.

In Mr. Lucas's memories of the meetings, he notes that political issues were not discussed; however, the meeting in itself was a political statement. A powerful figure like Mary McLeod Bethune didn't necessarily need to stand in a picket line to protest; rather, she used the place that she had ownership of—an institution of learning—to stand firm against injustice. She also allowed all of Daytona Beach and beyond to witness the jewel of performing arts and creativity that flowed throughout the community, and she was able to use that to gain necessary funding for the school. As a businesswoman, she was well aware of the wealth that the beach town generated, and she was able to shift tourism to an area of town where it was least expected. Throughout her lifetime, she continued to take a stand against the discriminatory nature of segregation. Her secretary, Mrs. Senorita Locklear, with whom she worked from 1954 to 1955, remembers Bethune's story of how she took a one-hour ride to the segregated Municipal Auditorium in Orlando to hear a noted speaker. Knowing the policies (most likely before she took the trip), when she arrived, she went straight to the front section that was designated for whites. When the usher informed her that the section was for whites only, pointing to the sign, she said, "I know, I can read." And she didn't budge.

In an interview with Mrs. Virginia Foster Durr, a civil rights activist and close friend of first lady Eleanor Roosevelt, Durr remembered Bethune integrating a hotel in Greensboro, North Carolina. The women worked together in the Southern Conference for Human Welfare, an interracial conference that lasted from 1938 to 1948 and sought to extend New Deal reform to southern states. Ending poll taxes, which restricted black voters, was a major aim of the conference. During the 1938 meeting in Birmingham,

Alabama, First Lady Roosevelt defied police orders and sat in the middle of the aisles, thereby integrating the separated audience. Although she risked being arrested, she made a statement that she was not moved by the policies of segregation. During that same meeting, when Bethune was called by her first name when it was her time to take the microphone, she corrected the speaker, reintroducing herself as "Mrs. Bethune." More than thirty-five years after that moment, Durr remembered how profound it was, saying, "So, Louise Charlton had to say 'Mrs. Bethune, will you come to the platform.' Well, that sounds like a small thing now, but that was a big dividing line. A Negro woman in Birmingham, Alabama, called 'Mrs. Bethune' at a public meeting. So Mrs. Bethune was very eloquent as always." She also remembered having a meeting in which black members of the conference were told that they would be escorted away from the hotel for lunch at the local black school. Bethune would not accept the humiliating experience of having to exit for lunch. Durr remembered the situation vividly:

> She said, "Now look, Jim Dombrowski, when you arrange a meeting, you arrange for us to eat together. We are not going to be shunted off this way." Oh, she got very upset about it, and poor Jim was just terribly upset. But Mrs. Bethune refused to go over to the black school to eat. I said, "Mrs. Bethune, you come on up to my room, and I will get you a sandwich." I wanted her to lie down because she was an old lady and…she didn't have an asthma attack that time, but she was pretty agitated and got everybody else pretty agitated, too. Mrs. Bethune could make the most marvelous speech about black roses. You've never heard her rose garden speech? About how she went into this lovely rose garden, and there was a pink rose and a yellow rose and a white rose and the red rose, and then one day, she went into the garden, and there was a black rose, the most beautiful rose of all. She was a masterful orator. She was an amazing woman. So, I took her up to my room, and she lay down on the bed and I called down to the dining room and asked if I could have lunch sent down to the room. And they said yes. So, I asked for two chicken sandwiches and two glasses of iced tea. Well, in about five minutes, here come in three black waiters, not one but three. They set up a table, put on a white cloth and set it beautifully, and then they brought up the chicken salad sandwiches and the iced tea, and they stayed and served Mrs. Bethune and me, one behind each chair and one to serve. [Laughter.] They were trying to show Mrs. Bethune honor, you see. This was their way of showing her honor, and they did. And she sat there like a queen and ate her sandwich and drank her iced tea, and these three

black waiters were just bowing and scraping. She was a powerful woman, I'm telling you. She broke segregation in that hotel, too. That's the second time that she did it. She didn't let anybody fool around with her.

As Bethune openly used her school and her influence to publicly protest segregation, she taught students to challenge the system through interracial cooperation. In March 1939, B-CC students hosted an interracial discussion on the problems of youth. Students from the white institutions Rollins College and Florida Southern College (Lakeland) attended, led by instructor Dr. Edwin L. Clarke. Students from HBCUs (historically black colleges/universities) included Edward Waters College (Jacksonville) and Florida Normal and Industrial Institute (St. Augustine), known today as Florida Memorial University. The discussion had grown out of a previously held yearly conference on race relations between B-CC and Rollins. Over 50 students joined the 225 B-CC attendees as they discussed issues including politics, employment and professional development. During the day, students were hosted by B-CC and treated to lunch, and Bethune greeted attendees and gave a welcome address. Again, just as Sunday Community Meetings demonstrated that she would not accept the insult of segregation on her campus, this hosting of an interracial discussion shows that she was passing down the same bold stance to her students. The discussion on issues facing youths of both races brought commonalities that transcended race to the forefront to allow racial cooperation in figuring out how to resolve the issues together. In Florida in 1939, not practicing segregated seating in an interracial setting was a political statement: segregation was not allowed in Bethune's domain.

DEPART TO SERVE THE LOCAL COMMUNITY

For many African Americans, accessing adequate medical care was a challenge during segregation. African Americans were more likely than whites to die from illnesses such as tuberculosis in rural areas because of lack of access to state-issued treatments. It was not until the 1950s that southern medical schools admitted African American students. HBCUs, including the Howard University School of Medicine (located in Washington, D.C., and established in 1868) and Meharry Medical College (located in Nashville, Tennessee, and established in 1876), provided vital programs for African

McLeod Hospital in 1916. *Courtesy of the Bethune-Cookman University Archives.*

A Daytona Industrial School nursing student visiting a patient in the community in 1917. *Courtesy of the Bethune-Cookman University Archives.*

Americans seeking to go into the field as doctors. In rural Daytona, Bethune felt the lack of access to medical treatment firsthand when one of her students was stricken with appendicitis. She attempted to take the student to the local hospital and was turned away. Fortunately, after much convincing, Bethune was able to obtain medical treatment for the young lady. After realizing that the incident could have been fatal, she decided to start her very own hospital on the campus of the all-girls school. In 1911, the McLeod Hospital opened, and it was named in honor of her parents, Patsey and Samuel McLeod. A local graduate of Meharry Medical College, Texas Adams, was selected to be the doctor for the facility, which operated out of a small two-story cottage.

McLeod Hospital was the first black hospital in Daytona Beach, and it was also one of the only places in Volusia County to provide training for African American nurses through the establishment of the McLeod Training School for Nurses. In the early years, the hospital was a critical space in the community and gave medical access to those who might not otherwise have had it. According to Dr. Shelia Flemming's text *The Answered Prayer to a Dream*, "Between June 1914 and June 1915, the hospital staff cared for 105 patients, had 316 outpatients, made 242 community calls and performed 24 operations. The training school for nurses offered a three year academic program which included instructions in theoretical and practical knowledge in the medical, surgical, gynecological, and obstetrical nursing as well as childcare." The community calls sent nurses out into homes of the aged and poor to give them basic medical treatment, again providing critical access. The McLeod Hospital and the Training School were part of Bethune's commitment to serve the local community and to teach students the principles of the school's mission through firsthand involvement.

As the school continued to expand finances, challenges made maintaining the hospital out of reach for Mary. In 1931, after nearly two decades of management, Bethune, along with several other local community members, including Dr. Adams, petitioned the city for a black ward in the Halifax Hospital system. Initially, the city purchased her son Albert McLeod Bethune's hotel and converted it into a hospital. The facility was conveniently located on a property adjacent to the school on Second Avenue, which still allowed community members in Midtown easy access. Although it is unclear how much influence Bethune-Cookman College now had over the medical center, the nursing program at the school continued to graduate both women and men who would bridge the gap in medical access. In 1949, a separate annex was built for African Americans by the Halifax Hospital system.

Bethune's concern for the welfare of the community did not stop at medical treatment; she used the resources of her school to address any issues she felt needed resolving. To provide children in the community with access to a library, she started "The Around the World Story Hour" for children to come listen to stories read by the school's library staff. Hundreds of children—not only from Daytona Beach but also from across Volusia County—attended the weekly event. She believed that her school could be a beacon of hope to the black community, and because of its outreach programs, it was. Programs also included the Better Boys Club, which she established during the years of the all-girls school to provide positive programs for boys in the area. After noticing that many young men were hanging out and getting in trouble, Bethune decided to extend her reach beyond helping just girls to give boys an outlet. Noted Daytona Beach–born theologian Howard Thurman grew up as a member of the club and later recalled how it positively impacted his life.

As she promoted equality and access, Bethune also took on the issue of equal housing for the impoverished African Americans of Daytona Beach. Having grown up in rural South Carolina in a small cabin with no windows, she remembered what it was like to live in poverty. Fortunately, she was blessed with her own home, which included running water and electricity at a time when most of the community did not have access to either. She was gifted the home by the generosity of Mr. James Norris Gamble and Mr. Thomas White, but she never forgot where she came

Mary Bethune hosting a Mother's Day program at B-CC in 1918. *Courtesy of the Bethune-Cookman University Archives.*

Mary Bethune and Daytona Beach community leaders. *Courtesy of the Bethune-Cookman University Archives.*

Mary Bethune reading to a local community member. *Courtesy of the Bethune-Cookman University Archives.*

Opposite: Mary talking to local children. *Courtesy of the Bethune-Cookman University Archives.*

from and that others deserved the same opportunities to live well. In Daytona Beach, Bethune used her influence as president of Bethune-Cookman College to lobby for decent housing in the community. In 1938, she was selected to be the only African American member of the Daytona Beach Housing Board. From the beginning of her tenure, she pushed for housing that would be both affordable and suitable for the families in the area. As a result of her consistent efforts, funds were earmarked for new buildings, and in 1940, the Pine Haven Projects opened for African Americans. The projects were close to the B-CC campus and specifically offered public housing for low-income families.

Over the years, Mrs. Bethune took on the issue of equal housing as the president of the National Council of Negro Women by leading a postwar campaign under the slogan "Don't Rest Until Every Home Unfit for Human Habitation Is Stamped Out of Your City!" She also took on the issue of housing on a national scale when she made a statement before the Senate Banking and Currency Committee in 1945 expressing her discontentment with the Federal Housing Administration for its lack of assistance toward African Americans. Throughout her career, she always spoke out for accessibility to proper housing and the need for more of it. In Daytona Beach, she was able to see her vision come to fruition. In the spirit of the school's motto "Depart to Serve," Bethune was able to extend herself beyond the classroom and beyond the walls of B-CC to serve the community and the nation in areas that needed dire attention and interest.

GARNERING SUPPORT FOR EDUCATIONAL EQUALITY, THE WASHINGTON WAY

During a 1940 interview with Fisk president Dr. Charles Johnson, Bethune explained that she chose to start her school in Daytona, stating, "I think the educational situation of Florida and possibly of the lower East Coast is very vague. I went there because I was looking for a hard place to work." Seeing families relocating to take on the harsh work building railroads and understanding the violent nature of the political climate in the state, Bethune took on the task of building a school with a full understanding of what she would face. Much like her mentor Booker T. Washington, who founded Tuskegee Institute in 1881 in a shack in rural Alabama, she started with humble beginnings of $1.50. As lynchings occurred all over the nation, particularly in the South, Washington set out to start an industrial school to train African Americans in vocational skills, including construction, brickmaking, farming and dressmaking, that stressed the dignity of labor. Over the years, he solicited the support of the nation and even that of President Theodore Roosevelt, who invited him for a meal at the White House in 1901. Over the years, he traveled extensively, not only for fundraising purposes, but also to rally people of all races to support the education of African Americans.

In 1912, Washington dedicated a week to an educational campaign throughout the state of Florida, and it was then that Bethune was able to meet him and receive valuable mentorship. He traveled throughout the state to cities including Lake City, Lakeland, Jacksonville, Daytona Beach, Eatonville and Tallahassee. He visited Florida State Normal School, Robert Hungerford Normal and Industrial, Dunbar Graded School and various churches throughout the state. During his visits, he rallied people to support the educational endeavors of African Americans, spoke against lynching and called for better race relations throughout the state. Just weeks before his arrival in Lake City, six African American men had been hanged, and the community's racial tension was dangerously thick. Washington's visit was a timely one for both races. Often in speeches, he stressed the responsibilities of peaceful coexistence on the part of both races. He also encouraged African Americans to be thrifty and to take initiative in starting their own financial institutions. His meetings in Ocala resulted in the 1913 founding of the Metropolitan Savings Bank.

When Washington came to Daytona Beach, he spoke in the morning to African Americans at the First Presbyterian Church and later in the day to whites at a local Daytona Theater. During the afternoon, Bethune hosted a dinner and showed him the campus of the all-girls school. For her, it was important that he give her school the stamp of approval; after all, at the time he was the most influential African American leader and educator. During the short time he spent with Bethune, Washington shared invaluable insight on ways to garner more support from white philanthropists for fundraising purposes. For Bethune, it was a dream fulfilled. In a 1940 interview with Fisk University president Dr. Charles Johnson, she recalled having a dream in which Booker T. Washington gave her a diamond covered in a handkerchief to help start her school. To have the dream, possibly a decade before his arrival, and later have his support for her efforts in Daytona was both a point of pride and the culmination of possibility.

Although it was only a few years before Washington's untimely 1915 death, Bethune carried his model of industrial education to audiences through speeches and letter-writing campaigns for financial support. While her school also promoted liberal arts training, she utilized the popularity of industrial education to draw support. She also traveled extensively, just as Washington had done, to draw attention to the need for educational equality and to solicit assistance. In 1915, she invited the mayor and city commissioner of Daytona Beach to visit for inspection of the educational activities of the school, and the *Daytona Morning Journal* published a letter she wrote about the visit. In 1920, she wrote to the *New York Times* to garner support for the Daytona Normal and Industrial Institute for Negro Girls' work in training nurses and teaching Christian ideals and its role in "performing a duty for the white people."

Just as Booker T. Washington had shown white audiences how assisting with African American education programs would benefit them, Mary McLeod Bethune did the same. Her work caught the attention of National Association for the Advancement of Colored People (NAACP) leader and journalist William Pickens. In a 1921 article, "The Story of Mary McLeod Bethune Bares South's Educational 'Equality,'" he wrote about Volusia

County, Florida's $96,000 appropriation for white children versus the $12,000 appropriation for African American children. He also pointed out that Bethune's school filled the gap for students who might otherwise have been cheated by the underfunded school system, but for parents, private education presented an extra tax that would not have existed were there equal support of the schools. Challenging President Warren Harding to provide true educational equality, Pickens made the point that "separate but equal" was merely a statement that carried no weight.

For Bethune, the article not only showed the need for equality in education but also demonstrated how her school filled a void in the African American community by offering the quality education that America failed to provide. As she traveled about garnering support for her school, she continued to speak out against discrimination in educational resources. In a 1937 speech to a New York audience, she addressed how self-sufficiency within the race would save Bethune-Cookman College, the lack of accessibility to high school education throughout the state of Florida and the state's unfair spending of six times more on white children's education. The meeting was a part of a Bethune-Cookman College Campaign to raise money for the school, and Bethune enlisted the assistance of leading African Americans, including New York State tax commissioner Hubert Delaney (who would later become a New York judge) and New York State judge James Watson. She also enlisted the help of President Franklin D. Roosevelt's mother, Mrs. James Roosevelt, when she signed on to serve as the honorary chair of a $500,000 drive in 1936. During the fundraising drive hosted by Mrs. Roosevelt at her home, Bethune again made the point that inequality in resources for African American children hindered the success of the community. Influential attendees, including United States senator and B-CC trustee Frederic C. Walcott, lauded Bethune for her work as a "racial harmonizer" who had given African Americans unique opportunities. Again, she was able to build on the ideals passed on to her by Booker T. Washington, not only advocating on her own for the cause of education but also surrounding herself with influential people who would do so as well.

Bethune worked with other HBCUs to eliminate economic equalities, and on April 25, 1944, she joined Tuskegee Institute president Dr. Frederick D. Patterson to organize the United Negro College Fund (UNCF). The UNCF sought to raise money by making an "appeal to the national conscience" and was able to garner the support of John D. Rockefeller Jr. and President Franklin D. Roosevelt, both of whom were good friends of Bethune's. Rockefeller served as chairman of UNCF's National

Council from 1944 to 1959. In its initial year, twenty-seven colleges joined, including Spelman College, LeMoyne-Owen College, Bennett College, Fisk University, Morehouse College and Wiley College. On its first drive, UNCF organization raised $760,000 (equating to over $8,000,000 in 2015). By November 1944, the fund raised $901,812, almost reaching its goal of $1,500,000. According to the report by national chairman Walter Hoving, "Corporations gave $228,831 and foundations gave $113,055…Negroes themselves contributed upward of $100,000. Of this amount $35,948 came from Negro service men, most of them overseas."

As separate and unequal funding across the United States limited the reach of HBCUs, they continued to find new ways to break the barriers of economic discrimination. UNCF brought interracial support to colleges that created African American leaders and educators. It is important to note that men serving overseas during the 1944 year were fighting World War II for the "Double V," victory abroad and victory at home, and certainly UNCF was an important part of their struggle for equality. Over the years, Bethune continued to support UNCF, oftentimes using her influence to encourage philanthropists to support the fundraising drives. In her April 2, 1949 *Chicago Defender* article, she highlighted the story of the founding of member college Lincoln University in hopes of gaining support from her readers. After fully retiring as president of B-CC and the National Council of Negro Women, she became one of four board directors of UNCF in 1952. For Bethune, the organization was yet another way to defeat the odds against her.

RALLYING BLACK VOTERS

Bethune did not limit herself in the role of college president, and she was quite politically active in Florida, with the school serving as the center of activism. After the ratification of the Nineteenth Amendment in 1920, which gave women the right to vote, Bethune was adamant about African American women using the ballot as a means to create change. She once told an audience, "Eat your bread without butter, but pay your poll tax! Nobody ever told me to pay my poll tax. My dollar is always there on time." Stories of Bethune riding her bike across town to collect money to pay poll taxes show her fierce determination to vote.

In 1920, she rallied African Americans, particularly women in Daytona Beach, to vote. According to scholar Dr. Paul Ortiz in his book *Emancipation*

Betrayed, Bethune utilized her school as a space to bring together black ministers and activists to strategize about how to get the community to practice voting. She also held night classes for local community members, teaching them to read in order to pass literacy tests for voting. But before voting took place, the KKK orchestrated a power outage on the campus of the all-girls school and came to the campus to confront Bethune for her efforts in galvanizing black voters. When they arrived and encircled the campus dorms, she was ready and had nearly 150 students come out to sing, "Be not dismayed whate'er betide—God Will Take Care of You." She switched on the lights with the help of her generator. The next day, Bethune arrived at the polls bright and early and made it her duty to walk up and down the voting lines to encourage black voters to stay in the lines even though they moved much slower than lines for whites. She was not deterred, and due to her activism, "Daytona city precinct witnessed a record turnout: at least 453 African American women—well over half of the adult black female population—and 167 black men registered to vote, giving African Americans a strong voting presence in Daytona," according to Ortiz. Over the years, Bethune continued to vote but was a staunch activist in the anti-poll tax movement, particularly in her role as vice-president of the Southern Conference for Human Welfare. The organization fought heavily against discrimination at the voting polls.

In 1948 (at the age of seventy-three), toward the end of her life, Bethune used her position as "First Lady of Negro America" to again rally black voters. A close friend of hers, George Engram, was running for city commissioner. Although threat letters piled up on her desk and, in her words, despite the "desperate challenge of the Klan," she made radio speeches on his behalf and put her full support behind George Engram. In her *Chicago Defender* column about the historic occasion of a black man running for city commissioner, she wrote:

> *I have waited long years to see George Engram, a well prepared young Negro resident run with five white men for the important office of Commissioner of the city! White Daytona was dumbfounded! They could not believe their eyes and ears but Negroes, well schooled in political unity here over a long period of time stood firmly together.*

Although Engram did not win the election, losing by a narrow margin of seven hundred votes, Bethune counted it as a success. She stated, "It is revealed in this incident Negroes are no longer afraid. They are on the march and for them there will always be next time at the polls." For her, it was a win because black Daytona made a statement that it would not be dismayed or afraid to use the ballot to address issues in the community. Again, she had extended herself and sacrificed her personal safety for the sake of rallying voters to create change.

AN HONOR IN HER HOME STATE

On February 22, 1949, Mary McLeod Bethune became the first African American to receive an honorary degree from a southern white educational institution. Not far from home in Daytona Beach, she was awarded a doctorate of humane letters from Rollins College in Winter Park, Florida. President Hamilton Holt broke southern tradition by honoring a woman he had known and respected as an educator and activist. Founded in 1885, Rollins College is the oldest institution of higher education in the state of Florida. Incorporated in 1887, initially Winter Park included a racially mixed town council, but within the next five years, the white residents of the town broke off into their own community. It was only when Winter Park needed more citizens to accept federal funding that it agreed to re-annex the African American community of Hannibal Square back into the town. Rollins College was segregated, just as the town was, and did not accept African American students until the late 1960s.

The honorary degree from Rollins College was the tenth for Bethune but her first from a non–African American institution. In 1910, she received her first honorary master's of science from South Carolina State College. Other degrees included doctor of law degrees from Lincoln University (1935), Howard University (1942), Atlanta University (1943) and Wiley College (1943). For her, the honorary degree from Rollins College was particularly important because it was recognition from the state she called home and because of its symbolism in the harsh racial climate of Florida. Winter Park was a typical segregated town. Just fifteen years before receiving the honorary degree, Holt had invited Bethune to come speak to the students of Rollins College and was informed by the board that if she came, he would no longer be president. Faced with an ultimatum, he apologetically explained the situation to Bethune, and she insisted that he should not put his presidency on the line. For her, the personal friendship she had developed with and the interracial work that they would do together was more important than the speaking engagement.

A founding member of the National Association for the Advancement of Colored People (NAACP), Hamilton Holt supported the ideals of racial equality and was an advocate for international peace. During his tenure at Rollins, there were incidents in which he would have been faced with possible racial uproar if he had allowed his ideals to prevail. In 1947, Rollins College's homecoming football game was canceled when the school became aware of an African American player, Kenneth Woodward, on the opposing team, Ohio Wesleyan University. The school was informed that there would be a major uproar if the game were played, particularly since it was being held at Orlando Stadium. After the incident, Holt called a meeting with the faculty and students and explained:

> *May I say this to you students; you will probably have critical decisions like this to make as you go through life—decisions that whatever you do, you will be misinterpreted, misunderstood, and reviled…It seemed to all of us that our loyalties to Rollins and its ideals were not to precipitate a crisis that might and probably would promote bad race relations, but to work quietly for better race relations, hoping and believing that time would be on our side.*

Although he may have felt that the game should have occurred, he chose to take a stance against policies of segregation in other ways. In that same year, he selected African American housemaid Susan Wesley to receive the Decoration of Honor for servicing the school's freshmen dorm for over twenty years. Having Susan on the commencement platform was the first time the school had allowed an African American to appear there. That year (1947), Dr. Holt's plan was to honor Mrs. Bethune, but he was prevented from doing so by the board of trustees. The following year, knowing that the board was against the idea, he honored her with the doctorate during the mid-winter convocation for the school. Recalling the incident fifteen years earlier when she was not allowed to speak at the school, one would imagine that Bethune most likely felt as though she had slowly knocked down another layer of racism. During that time, such an honor was unheard of in the South, and the *Chicago Defender* called it "a milestone in human relations." The African American community celebrated, and she shared her appreciation through her weekly column in the *Defender*, where she wrote that she was proud and honored to be selected. That same year, Dr. Holt retired from his presidency, but his last commencement was remembered as the one in which he gave due credit to the activism and trailblazing record of Mary McLeod Bethune.

A SPACE OF INTERNATIONALISM

In August 1949, after arriving back from a ten-day trip to Haiti, where she'd received the coveted Haitian Medal of Honor, Mary McLeod Bethune shared her feelings about the country in the *Chicago Defender*: "I LOVE HAITI! I LOVE HER PEOPLE!" The educator, political activist and organizer had fallen in love with the First Black Republic. Throughout her lifetime, Bethune created a legacy of unity and cultural exchange between people of African descent that would be illustrated through her travels, and she sought to bring that spirit of purpose-driven internationalism back to Daytona Beach, particularly to her school. She often invited political figures from various countries across the world to engage the local community and to bring more cultural awareness to the audience. Located in central Florida, Daytona Beach does not offer the cultural diversity of southern Florida cities.

Frank Guridy's book *Forging Diaspora* speaks of relations between African Americans and Afro-Cubans in the late 1800s and early 1900s. The text demonstrates how Booker T. Washington's Tuskegee Institute became a melting pot for Afro-Cuban, African American and Puerto Rican students. Washington's autobiography, *Up from Slavery*, also appealed to Afro-Cubans through its theme of racial uplift. After the translation of the text to Spanish, "thousands of letters from students and their parents throughout the African Diaspora expressing their interest in attending Tuskegee" essentially made Tuskegee a successful diasporic space. Following in the footsteps of her mentor, during the time of Bethune's tenure and even afterward, Bethune-Cookman welcomed Cuban students and professors into its tight community. In the school's 1950–51 annual catalogue, *The Advocate*, listed among its academic students was Pedro P. Portuondo from Havana, Cuba. The 1954 *B-Cean* school yearbook featured visitors from Cuba during the school year and Cuban students, including Gloria del Pozo from Havana.

Even after experiencing disappointing discrimination during a trip to Cuba in 1930, Bethune continued to dedicate herself to stronger relationships between Cubans and Americans, particularly Afro-Cubans and African Americans. In November 1950, she spoke at the Cuban American Goodwill Association Banquet. Founded by Henry Grillo and Pedro Portuondo Calá, the organization "promoted cultural exchanges between Afro-Cubans and African Americans" and assisted in tour opportunities for travelers. Bethune encouraged the organization during its first annual banquet to continue its work. She also emphasized the importance of such an organization: "We must know each other, love one another, build each other up and encourage one another." Other supporters in attendance included Nora R. Tucker, who also called for better relations between the "darker people" of Cuba and America. Lending her voice to the association in support of its attempts to bring about closer relations between Afro-Cubans and Cubans speaks to her role as a supporter to those who organized under the guise of Pan-Africanism.

Bethune's close relationship with Henry Grillo had begun during his tenure as a student. In *Black Cuban, Black American: A Memoir*, written by Henry's brother Evelio Grillo, Evelio noted that Henry "becomes very close to Mary McCloud Bethune while at Bethune Cookman." In 1930, Henry was in Bethune-Cookman's Junior High School class, serving as a business manager for his class, as music editor for the school's Wildcat yearbook staff and as a member of the Tampa Club. Although it is unclear if Henry graduated from Bethune-Cookman, he did manage to stay in contact with Bethune and volunteered in the National Youth Administration during her tenure as director of Negro affairs. In a 1954 photo of Henry Grillo as an adult, along with Bethune and her great-grandson Donald Bethune pictured at Mary's home, on the back of the photo he wrote: "To Mother Dear: Just reminding you that the Grillos will continue your good work for many years to come. Your boys, Rafael and Henry, May 20, 1954." What started as a student-teacher relationship resulted in a partnership in which Bethune used her influence to promote the work of the Cuban American Goodwill Association to bring unity between African Americans and Afro-Cubans—and it all started at B-CC.

BAHAMAS

In an article in the *Chicago Defender* on May 9, 1953, Bethune encouraged readers to build friendships with the people of the Bahamas and to "stretch our hands across the waters." She was a sought-after speaker and advisor to organizations and universities, and Emerald Nicholls and the Carver Garden Club invited her to Nassau, Bahamas, to inspire the newly organized suffragists. During the trip, she also addressed several Bahamian women who had been part of the five-year push to be franchised. With the founding of the National Council of Negro Women in 1935 and her push for equal voting rights for African Americans, she brought much experience and zeal to the island. Bethune attended conferences while on the island and strategized and made several suggestions "pertaining to the growth and improvement of Nassau." She spoke to the women of the Carver Garden Club, encouraging them to commit to serving the community and continuing to work to "break down the barriers which have been erected by those who believe that we lack adequate preparation."

Bethune's charge to build bonds with Bahamians was implemented in Bethune-Cookman during and after her tenure. By 1948, the school had enrolled students from "Africa, Nassau, and Honduras," according to the *Daytona Beach Morning Journal*. In the 1952 student register, Elsa L. Ingraham and John Howard Storr from Nassau, Bahamas, were listed as students. In the 1954 *B-Cean* yearbook, Nassau's governor general is pictured attending a Bethune-Cookman tennis tournament. After her 1955 death, Bahamian students continued to attend the university. In 1968, Miss Carolyn Scott and Mr. Rodney E.C. Johnson, two students from Nassau, received the Winn-Dixie scholarship to further their education at the school. The alumni of Bethune-Cookman traveled to the Bahamas for four days in 1965. During the trip, they met government officials, were hosted by the Bahamas Mothers Club and were able to learn about the history and culture of the island. In 1970, several students arrived at the Daytona Beach Municipal Airport to meet Lynden Pindling, the prime minister of the Bahamas. Bethune-Cookman president Dr. Richard V. Moore was also in attendance and "welcomed [Pindling] to participate in activities of Bethune-Cookman's Honors Convocation."

United Nations

In May 1945, Bethune accepted the honor to serve with NAACP members Walter White and W.E.B. Dubois, making history as the only African American woman to serve as an associate consultant for the founding charter of the United Nations. From April 25 to June 26, 1945, delegates from fifty countries held sessions to create the foundations of the United Nations. In May, at the San Francisco conference, Bethune hit the ground running with the NAACP and its main objective to address the issues of colonialism and discrimination. White, Bethune and Dubois sent a letter to Edward Stettinius, the chairman of the American delegation, critiquing the proposals. Chapter 1, paragraph 3, of the declaration called for human rights and freedom from discrimination; however, the consultants pointed out that it left out "the mass of people living in colonies, against whom discrimination is customary and unjustifiable." They also criticized the conference for denying representation to the countries that the United Nations had taken under colonial trusteeship. They argued that it was "unthinkable that the mandated colonies distributed after the First World War should be returned to the position of colonies owned by other countries." Working together, the trio called for those under the colonial system to obtain autonomy through revision of the declaration.

In his recap of their representation, Walter White wrote in the *Chicago Defender*, "The consultants were a unit of insistence on the speediest possible abolition of colonial and all its evils." Although the three had followed very different political careers and were from different social/economic backgrounds, they put all of their differences aside at the San Francisco conference to stand united against colonialism. White spoke highly of the differences in the presentations but the powerful impact they'd left, writing that Dubois presented facts on colonial exploitation while Bethune "made a stirring plea at one session for the disadvantaged people of the earth, particularly American Negroes." Utilizing her experiences as the leader of the National Youth Administration's Division of Negro Affairs, founder of the NCNW, member and past president of NACW and president of the Association for the Study of Negro Life and History (ASNLH), she was well equipped to discuss the discrimination and inequalities faced by African Americans. Although the group did not obtain the expected outcome, Bethune's activism toward liberation continued and was taken to a greater level following the conference.

On October 24, 1945, the United Nations Charter was ratified, and the United Nations came into existence without the complete abolishment of colonialism. Although the Declaration on the Granting of Independence to Colonial Countries and Peoples was not adopted by the United Nations until December 14, 1960, Bethune and the NCNW continued to push for true democracy for colonized countries and an end to discrimination. The NCNW's report on the United Nations offered suggestions for how the council could create change as a member of the United Nations and connect with those outside the United States. During the sessions, Bethune and Madame Vijayalakshmi Pandit found a connection in their struggles for equality and liberation, and the pair became close friends. As India was in the midst of its struggle for freedom from the British, Pandit had traveled to the United States as a diplomat and was able to attend the San Francisco conference.

Upon returning to her home in Daytona Beach, Florida, Bethune shared her experiences with the local African American community. In a discussion at Bethune-Cookman College, she spoke to students and community members. Expressing her disappointment in the United States' delegation, she stated that one of its mistakes was "the failure of the U.S. to assume leadership in the matter of representing 750,000,000 colonial people who had no voice in the gathering." At the time, all of Africa was ruled by colonial forces, with the exception of Liberia and Ethiopia, severely limiting the independence of the continent. Bethune told her audience that her position at the conference had been to represent both colonial people and African Americans, whom she felt were in a similar condition because they were "not permitted to exercise their rights under the constitution of the U.S." In this comparison, Mrs. Bethune recognized that although African Americans lived in a free country, they were in no way freer than Africans living in the colonies. As a person who had studied the conditions and worked with local communities to better their positions, she was well aware of what African Americans faced. She urged the Daytona Beach audience to prepare and become aware of the issues faced, stating, "Do your part. Study, become skilled, be able to stand on your feet." She utilized her experience and her disappointment with the U.S. delegation to rally African Americans to do their part in changing the situation.

Mary Bethune and Vijayalakshmi Pandit of India on the campus of Bethune-Cookman College. *Courtesy of the Bethune-Cookman University Archives.*

Mary McLeod Bethune in Florida

In 1951, Madame Vijayalakshmi Pandit addressed hundreds of B-CC students and faculty and Daytona Beach community members about "her personal fight for the release of her people and her determination to release mankind the world over." She had been heavily involved in the Indian independence movement for freedom from the British, often serving time in jail for her political beliefs. As two women working in a male-dominated atmosphere and trying to insert freedom into a conversation of imperialism, Bethune and Pandit made a connection that not only brought them into a friendship but also built a bridge between African Americans and the women of India. Pandit brought philosophies of the nonviolent leader Mahatma Gandhi to her Daytona Beach audience by spreading his message of equality among Indians and essentially among all people. In her message at B-CC, she infused her past experiences as a freedom fighter to give the community a snapshot of what it would take to liberate those still in bondage to colonialism. She also encouraged her audience to "remain steadfast in the fight for freedom, for brotherhood—for security," which made a strong statement against the system of Jim Crow. Among the few female delegates at the founding of the United Nations, Indian ambassador Pandit and Bethune quickly developed a good friendship, and Pandit brought her story of activism to share with the people of Daytona Beach.

B-CC Representation in Liberia

In 1895, Bethune graduated from Moody Bible Institute. She applied to become a missionary with the Presbyterian Mission Board of New York. From an early age, hearing her minister speak of the need to go to Africa, she had set her sights on doing so and, in her words, "had a yearning to go to Africa." In a 1940 interview of Bethune and Dr. Charles S. Johnson, she stated that her mother had "came down from one of the great royalties of Africa," recalling knowledge of family connections to the continent. Bethune's dreams were shattered when she was denied the opportunity to serve as a missionary, and she was most likely among many African Americans who were not permitted to go to Africa. In Bettye Collier-Thomas's text *Jesus, Jobs, and Justice: African American Women and Religion*, she explains that the number of African American missionaries sharply declined in the early 1900s. With the Berlin Conference occurring in 1884–85, resulting in the colonization of most of Africa, "the rise of the 'New Negro' consciousness, Pan-Africanism, Marcus Moziah Garvey and the Universal Negro Improvement Association's Back to

Africa Movement, [along with] other ideologies among African Americans, were threatening to European colonial powers." The radical ideas of African Americans would weaken the hold of Europeans; therefore, many were prohibited from going altogether. Although Bethune was not able to make the voyage to Africa until 1952, she did not forget her African lineage, and she continued to try to extend her reach to Africa. In later years, from across the seas, she received letters of admiration and love from people of African descent, and she cherished those letters. She took the concerns of the people into consideration as she went about her work with the United Nations and as she led NCNW. The bulk of her activism was done in the United States, but she was known internationally for the strides she was making toward equality for people of African descent.

In December 1946, Lamar Fort arrived in Liberia to take on the position of agricultural production specialist with the United States Economic Mission. Before taking the position, Fort was Bethune-Cookman College's director of agriculture, where he worked under Bethune's leadership. The mission would become part of the Foreign Operations Administration, a program designed to provide "cooperative development of economic and military strength among the nations of the free world." The program was part of a United States effort to create allies against the Soviet Union during the Cold War. During his tenure, Lamar "trained several hundred Liberians in the use of improved farm practices" and helped expand the trade of cocoa between the United States and Liberia.

While in Liberia, Fort often wrote to Bethune, updating her on his work in Liberia and inquiring about the status of students and faculty at Bethune-Cookman. In his May 15, 1947 letter, he wrote to her from Cape Palmas, Liberia, explaining that much of his current work was dedicated to finding natural resources. Fort also wrote that as a part of his economic mission, he was traveling throughout Liberia to create an updated map of the country. Although it is unclear whether Bethune assisted in securing the job for Fort, he was indebted to her. In his June 10, 1947 letter, he wrote, "I shall endeavor to do my best and not to let you down. After all, had you not had me at your college I never would have had this job. I feel exceedingly grateful to you for whatever I shall be able to accomplish." Given her position as a consultant to the founding of the United Nations and later a delegate to Liberia (both positions as a result of her close relationship with President Harry S. Truman), it is possible that Bethune's political connections assisted Fort in obtaining the job. Although he was working in Liberia on an economic mission, he also found time to promote Bethune-Cookman College, and in correspondence with her, he expressed plans to try to send more students to the college. He also wanted to make them aware of Bethune's work. His presence as a government official and former Bethune-Cookman faculty member allowed him to introduce her to Liberia as someone with whom he'd worked personally while also acting as a representative of the school. Through Fort's promotion of the school, Bethune's presence was felt in Liberia prior to her arrival.

Part II

Maintaining the Legacy of Mary Bethune at the Bethune Foundation Historic Home

O n March 17, 1953, Mary McLeod Bethune opened her home to establish the Mary McLeod Bethune Foundation. At the age of seventy-seven, she had accomplished much as a college president, women's rights organizer and presidential consultant, and the opening of the foundation was her last endeavor. Bethune saw the foundation as her way of inspiring others by sharing her life's work. Nestled in the heart of Midtown, Daytona Beach's flourishing black community, on the campus of Bethune-Cookman University, today her home has the honored distinction of being a National Historic Landmark, and thousands of visitors from around the world come here to walk in the steps of its founder.

Audrey Thomas McCluskey and Elaine M. Smith's text *Mary McLeod Bethune: Building a Better World* features a transcript of a 1954 interview of Bethune in her home discussing why she established the foundation. She stated:

> *So I want this to be kind of a sacred place—a place to awaken people and to have them realize that there is something in the world they can do; and if they try hard enough, they will do that thing. I thought that the money that would come in from others would be used for scholarships for leaders. I think we need leaders now so much. I thought that we would hold conferences, interracial conferences with women of all classes and creeds that we might sit together, think together, and plan together how we might make a better world to live in.*

Mary and male students in 1924, shortly after the merger with Cookman Institute. *Courtesy of the Bethune-Cookman University Archives.*

Mary giving a speech with Richard Moore and Texas Adams (seated). *Courtesy of the Bethune-Cookman University Archives.*

Opposite, top: Mary Bethune, Dr. Texas Adams (left) and Mr. M.S. Davage (right) celebrating Mary's seventy-third birthday. *Courtesy of the Bethune-Cookman University Archives.*

Opposite, bottom: Mary Bethune working as college president. *Courtesy of the Bethune-Cookman University Archives.*

Students making brooms during vocational class at B-CC. *Courtesy of the Bethune-Cookman University Archives.*

Then I thought that we would have a Finding Place here. [A]ll the material on my life that we could get our hands on would be placed so that those who want to write about me in the years to come could find that material here that would give them the information. I just want this to be a place for people.

THE RETREAT

In her letters to friends, Bethune often referred to the house as "The Retreat" because it was the comfortable place where she would retreat from the busyness of her life. Some also knew it as the "Bethune Mansion." An African American architect by the name of A.B. Raddick built the house around 1904–05. He also built homes for wealthy whites who lived on the beachside of Daytona Beach, and his home was thought of as a "model home" that showed off his skills. In 1913, the home was purchased for Bethune by Mr. James Norris Gamble, the chemist who devised the formula for ivory soap, and Mr. Thomas White of White Sewing Machine Company. Having grown up in a log cabin with boards for windows, she thought of the home as a gift from God. In a 1954 interview, she said, "When I wake up in the morning and look around, see my glass windows, I see my Bible on the table, see the rug on my floor, my bathroom, my bath tub, I have a thanksgiving in my heart for what God has done for me." Over the years, the home was where Bethune raised her son, grandson and great-grandson. As a mother, grandmother and foster mother, she opened her home to those closest to her and welcomed them to share what God had blessed her with. Her great-granddaughter Ms. Patricia Pettus remembered the home as a very fun place as a child:

> The foundation was not just the Foundation to me and my brothers, but it was a place where we played and grew up. Being that I was her first female off-spring, as her great-granddaughter, I was pampered and treated a little special by her. As the story was told by my father, I was her favorite! My most memorable moments were spent in her bedroom playing in her jewelry box. I remembered it being a place where we would spend quality time together.

Bethune opened her home not only to her family but also to various famous guests, including baseball great Jackie Robinson and Nobel Peace Prize winner Ralph Bunche. In 1931, Harlem Renaissance poet Langston Hughes visited the home after a trip to Miami. Not only did she allow him to stay with her, but she also convinced him to take a reading tour to historically black colleges throughout the South. In later accounts, he spoke highly of how she had welcomed and encouraged him during his trip to Daytona Beach. Even before she started the foundation, Bethune's home was a place where she met with leaders, discussed the issues of the day and mentored those who came seeking her tutelage and wise words.

The house was also a place of activism where Mrs. Bethune helped organize for equality in her local community. In 1949, Peabody Auditorium opened in Daytona Beach on the beachside, and although it was built with public tax dollars, the facility barred African American patrons. She met with local community leaders in her home to discuss plans to desegregate the facility, and as a result, the group sued the city to protest the ruling. The committee filing the suit was led by the Westside Business and Professional Men's Association, including the legal committee chairman G.D. Rogers; the organization's president, Herbert Thompson; secretary John Dickerson; and treasurer Clifford Jenkins. Although Bethune was not a part of the official suing of the city, she had organized the group in her home and provided a space for it to come together to strategize.

The rooms of the house tell a story of a woman who rose to become one of the most influential figures of her time yet continued to be humble enough to share her sacred space. There are three bathrooms, four bedrooms and a sunroom in the house, and the home was sizable for the time period in which Bethune lived. From the time that she moved in, she always had electricity and plumbing. James N Gamble and Thomas White fought the city commissioners for utilities since they did not come to the black areas of town. She was the first person in the community to get electricity and plumbing. The bathroom downstairs is where Bethune passed away quietly after having a heart attack. In the kitchen, she did not do a lot of cooking in her later years. Many of her meals were delivered from the cafeteria, or her niece, Ms. Georgia McLeod, did most of the cooking. The dining room was where she hosted many of her important guests and always had dinner at the table even when she was alone. The breakfast nook in the kitchen is where she ate her lunch and breakfast. Smothered chicken wings and grits was one of her favorite meals.

According to Bethune's last secretary, Ms. Senorita Locklear, every day she would read the Holy Bible and *The Upper Room* daily devotional before beginning work. On the desk, there is one of Mary's original Bibles, and the devotional is turned to the day she passed away (May 18, 1955). All of the books are original to the home and feature topics including Christian science, black history and world history. Mrs. Bethune was an avid reader. In 1940 and 1953, First Lady Roosevelt visited Bethune-Cookman to speak at the dedication of the Mary McLeod Bethune Foundation, and she slept in the guest room. During one of her visits, Bethune wanted to let the first lady use her bedroom for the night, but the Secret Service agreed that her room had too many windows and was unsafe, so she was relegated to the guest room. She used Bethune's huge bathroom to tidy up. According to Bethune's grandson Mr. Albert McLeod Bethune, Jackie Robinson and his wife, Rachel, slept in the guest room during one of their numerous visits to the campus. In 1954, Jackie was awarded an honorary degree from the college.

On May 18, 1955, Mrs. Bethune passed away quietly in her home after suffering from a heart attack. During the viewing services, her body was memorialized in the office space of the home, which was also the headquarters of the foundation. Nearly four thousand people came to pay their respects and visited the home to take one last glimpse of one of the nation's greatest leaders. Bethune's family members received guests and watched over her body as they waited for the day of the funeral. The funeral was held next door in the B-CC chapel, and her body was laid to rest on the grounds of the home. Today, the foundation continues to preserve the grave site and home of its founder.

FOUNDING OF THE BETHUNE FOUNDATION

On February 26, 1953, the articles of incorporation for the Mary McLeod Bethune Foundation were approved, and the following month, Bethune quickly began to bring her vision to fruition. For her, the foundation would be a way to preserve her legacy even in death, and the idea was very much ahead of her time. Everything that she owned and felt was of significance was in her home and would be part of the foundation.

The purpose of the foundation was multifaceted, which is reflective of Bethune's many activities and accomplishments as a clubwoman, civil rights activist, educator, businesswoman and mother. Preservation of her personal and organizational papers was a major part of the foundation's purpose. She had plans to build a fireproof attachment to the home before her death to make sure that the papers would be safe. Over the years, the papers were copied to reels and made available in libraries and archival centers across the world, including at the National Archives for Black Women's History and the Library of Congress. The original papers have since been moved to the Bethune-Cookman University Archives in the school's library. This collection, initially preserved by Bethune, captures the history of Bethune-Cookman College (B-CC) dating back to 1915, documents her role as a government administrator with the National Youth Administration and offers insight into her involvement as founder of the National Council of Negro Women. The papers provide a complete scope of her life.

Bethune also ensured that the foundation would have an educational component. Not only was it founded to be a research facility, but it was also responsible for publishing articles related to the work of its founder. The foundation would support the work of Bethune-Cookman College by providing academic scholarships for students. As president, Bethune was often away for long periods of time raising money, and she understood the toll that this took on her as a leader. Although she'd retired, she wanted to continue to assist with fundraising and providing vital funds for students; the foundation was a way to achieve this goal. In an interview, she stated, "I have always wanted to set up a foundation to benefit less fortunate students who have the will to learn. All my worldy gifts I have bequeathed to this project, and I hope to see the day when it will rank with the outstanding educational foundations. It can be done with God's help."

Life as an activist and leader did not stop when Mrs. Bethune retired from presidency roles with B-CC and the National Council of Negro Women. Although the foundation had been her home, it was also a place where she hosted dinners to discuss issues of the day and political figures from around the world. This was a usual occurrence in the home. With the foundation, Mary wanted to continue this tradition by establishing that the organization would promote and support goodwill on the local, national and international levels. It was to be a place that fostered interracial cooperation throughout the nation, as well as a place of diplomacy.

BRICK UPON BRICK

On March 17, 1953, Mrs. Bethune officially opened her home to the Mary McLeod Bethune Foundation with a grand dedication service. Under the slogan "Brick Upon Brick," she vowed to share her home to continue to build on her lifetime of service. Bethune invited friends from near and far to attend the momentous occasion. First Lady Eleanor Roosevelt would serve as the speaker for the event, and her arrival was the talk of Daytona Beach, drawing hundreds to wait for her at the Daytona Beach Airport. Bethune organized an official welcoming committee to meet the first lady upon arrival at the airport, complete with officials and her young granddaughter Patricia Bethune and Carol Robin Zeiger serving as flower girls welcoming the special guest. Bethune, along with B-CC president Richard V. Moore and founder of the United Beauty School Owners and Teachers' Association Marjorie Joyner, waited to greet the first lady.

The dedication services were hosted at the newly desegregated Peabody Auditorium on the beachside of Daytona Beach. Over two hundred people attended as the Bethune Foundation became a reality. In her keynote address, First Lady Roosevelt stated: "This foundation you are creating tonight, Mrs. Bethune, will be a potent example of democracy in the United States. What you have done will not only be of value here but will make headlines in India, Indonesia, South America and elsewhere in the world." Having worked with First Lady Roosevelt during her tenure as director of Negro Affairs under the Franklin D. Roosevelt administration, Bethune continued to partner with her on various efforts. The first lady often consulted with her, and in 1953, the pair made the front page of *Ebony* magazine, sitting together as friends. The first lady also assisted with raising funds for B-CC and was awarded with an honorary degree from the college in 1953. During the dedication address, she reflected on the relationship between Bethune and her late husband, stating, "I am thinking that my husband would have been so happy at what you have done on this day, Dr. Bethune. He felt your work was of great value and always said that you had done a remarkable piece of work for all young people during the Depression."

During the celebration, Bethune announced that she was gifting her home and all of its contents and personal papers, valued at $40,000, to the newly established organization. She was chosen as the organization's president, Roy S. McWilliams as vice-president, Julius Davison as treasurer, Paul W. Harvey as legal advisor, Maxwell W. Saxon as curator and Bertha L. Mitchell as secretary. Also, Albert M. Bethune Sr., Marjorie S. Joyner, Richard V. Moore and John Sengstacke were named as trustees. The organization's advisory board included Ralph Bunche, Minister Howard Thurman and Judge Hobson Reynolds.

THE WORK BEGINS

In 1935, Mary McLeod Bethune set out to create the National Council of Negro Women to serve as an umbrella organization for all black women's organizations. While she was the organization's president (1935–49), she also worked with the Roosevelt administration (1936–43) and was the president of Bethune-Cookman College until 1942, resuming the role again from 1946 to 1947. In 1949, she retired from all activities, but less than five years later she started the foundation, ending her retirement. Bethune immediately began to get to work on building and promoting her new institution. She met often with trustees in the foundation, and while she was away, secretary Bertha L. Mitchell handled affairs and answered correspondence relating to the foundation. She began to travel and spread the ideas of the foundation as she had once done for her school since its 1904 founding. While away, she left specific details for her secretary to handle communications and had Vice-President Roy S. McWilliams sign checks in her absence.

Bethune's fundraising efforts were not in vain. During the first year of the foundation's existence, from March 1953 to March 1954, the foundation's total contributions were $14,716.50, with $2,821.00 raised in the first month. Supporters donated from across the nation, with gifts coming from places like Daytona Beach; Detroit; New York; Washington, D.C.; Pittsburgh; Minneapolis; and Houston. A donation was also sent from Monrovia, Liberia, where Bethune had traveled in 1952. Both individuals and businesses donated, including the News-Journal Corporation, King Features Syndicate, Sears-Roebuck Company and businessman Marshall Field. The largest donations were sent by Webber College ($1,000), Mr. Clifford M. Babson and Mrs. Nora M. Doughtry ($1,000), Mrs. Lillian Padget Hobson ($2,000) and Roger Babson ($1,000).

Among the biggest supporters of the foundation were Marjorie Joyner and the Alpha Chi Pi Omega Sorority. During the first year, the sorority and its founder donated the largest amount and the most number of times, totaling $4,106 donated over six different transactions. Marjorie Joyner hailed from

Mary Bethune, Marjorie Joyner and the women of Alpha Pi Chi Omega sorority for beauticians in the 1940s. *Courtesy of the Bethune-Cookman University Archives.*

Above: Trustees of the Bethune Foundation (1953). *From left to right*: Edward Rodriguez, Marjorie Joyner, Rickard V. Moore and George Engram. *Courtesy of the Bethune-Cookman University Archives.*

Right: Mary in the Mary McLeod Bethune Foundation headquarters office in her home in 1953. *Courtesy of the Bethune-Cookman University Archives.*

Chicago and was a very well-known entrepreneur and a pioneer in the beauty and cosmetology field. She was a stylist to the stars, including Marian Anderson and Billie Holiday. In her earlier years, Joyner had worked her way up the ranks with self-made millionaire beautician Madame C.J. Walker as a sales agent, and by 1919 she was a national secretary for Walker. For decades, she continued to work for Walker's company and developed a permanent wave machine, making her an inventor as well. In 1945, Joyner and Bethune co-founded the United Beauty School Owners and Teachers' Association. In the same year, she also created the Alpha Chi Pi Omega Sorority, which was the first sorority for beauticians. The sorority sought to standardize beauty practices and raise the level of professionalism for beauticians. Bethune served as one of the national sponsors and provided conference space for the sorority and association's national meetings at Bethune-Cookman College. She also opened her home to host a special reception for Joyner and sorority members. Members would visit the home to socialize and seek council from Bethune. During the 1953 dedication services for the foundation, Joyner was part of the welcoming committee for First Lady Roosevelt, and members of her organization also joined in the celebration of Bethune's new endeavor. Over the years, the sorority continued to pledge its support to the foundation and provided critical funds to help carry out its mission. Joyner also served as a trustee on the foundation's board.

OFF TO A GREAT START

The Mary McLeod Bethune Foundation immediately began the work of promoting the organization and sharing Bethune's work. On May 10, 1953, another dedication at the home was hosted on the lawn. B-CC played a major part in making the program a success. The B-CC choir provided music, and a plaque was given to the foundation by current president Dr. Moore while students gave tours.

It is important to note that tours began in 1953, as it shows the transition of Bethune's home from a private space to the museum/historic home–type setting that we know the foundation to be today. There was also a guest book for visitors to sign to document who had taken part in the event and the tours. In the first year, the guest books registered guests who came for tours, events in the home or to meet with Mary from thirty-four states, including Arizona, California, Missouri, Ohio, Tennessee, Texas and South Dakota.

There were also a number of international visitors from Canada, the United Kingdom, Germany, Japan, Bahamas, Cuba, Sierra Leone, Liberia and Kenya. Indeed, in its first year, the foundation had also become a museum open for tours.

Mrs. Bethune also continued to open her home to her friends who would come visit. Houseguests in the foundation's first year, some of whom had visited before 1953, included First Lady Roosevelt, famed contralto Marian Anderson, Nobel Peace Prize winner Ralph Bunche and assistant secretary of defense James C. Evans. *Ebony* magazine also covered the founding of the foundation and sent employee Allen Morrison to write the story; he stayed in the home during his visit. The list of famed visitors also included writers Ralph Ellison and Langston Hughes. International dignitaries who visited included governor of the Bahamas Robert Neville and Ernest J. Yancey, who served as secretary of public instruction in Monrovia, Liberia. Organizations came to talk with Bethune about her aims and goals for the foundation. Members of NCNW also visited and pledged financial support, while Arnetta G.

Wallace, president of Alpha Kappa Alpha Sorority Inc., paid a visit. Essentially, the foundation opened its doors as a source of inspiration, allowing people to take a firsthand look at what it took to accomplish one's goals. The home displays pictures of the cabin where Bethune grew up, showing her humble beginnings, while the awards, citations and the entire campus of B-CC provided clear evidence of what hard work can turn into. Also, having Bethune in the foundation and sharing moments with her was an opportunity to gain valuable counsel from a woman who advised presidents, started a thriving educational

Mary Bethune opening the Bethune Foundation in 1953. *Courtesy of the Bethune-Cookman University Archives.*

The Bethune Foundation/Home in 1940. *Courtesy of the Bethune-Cookman University Archives.*

institution and navigated through the Jim Crow South. The foundation became a haven for leaders and great thinkers and a place for Bethune to pass the torch of knowledge in her last years.

The work of the foundation also extended its reach outside the walls of the home. During its first year, Bethune wrote fifty-two articles for the *Chicago Defender* through her weekly column and an article for the daily devotional, *The Upper Room*. The foundation also served in advisory roles for several organizations, including the National Share Croppers and the National Association for the Advancement of Colored People. Scholarships funds in the amount of $500 were appropriated for the Mary McLeod Bethune Foundation Award to Bethune-Cookman College during the first year.

THE LEGACY CONTINUES

After Bethune's 1955 death, the foundation continued to flourish as a historic home to inspire others, as she hoped it would. On December 2, 1974, the home received historic recognition from the National Park Service and was added to the National Register of Historic Places (NRHP) and listed as a National Historic Landmark (NHL). According to the National Park Service:

> *The National Register of Historic Places is the official list of the Nation's historic places worthy of preservation. Authorized by the National Historic Preservation Act of 1966, the National Park Service's National Register of Historic Places is part of a national program to coordinate and support public and private efforts to identify, evaluate, and protect America's historic and archeological resources.*

The National Park Service defines a National Historic Landmark as "a historic building, site, structure, object, or district that represents an outstanding aspect of American history and culture." In order to qualify for this designation, the site must demonstrate one of the following characteristics:

- Be a location with the strongest association with a turning point or significant event in our nation's history.
- Be the best location to tell the story of an individual who played a significant role in the history of our nation.
- Be an exceptional representation of a particular building type, a building or engineering method/technique or an outstanding work of a nationally significant architect or engineer.
- Provide the potential to yield new and innovative information about the past through archaeology.

Both designations are awarded by the National Park Service after a nomination and application process. Once a site receives the status of NHL, it is automatically added to the NRHP. There are over 2,500 NHLs across the nation, including the Tuskegee Institute National Historic Site (Tuskegee, Alabama), Woodrow Wilson House (Washington, D.C.), Madame C.J. Walker Building (Indianapolis, Indiana) and the Robert Frost Homestead (Derry, New Hampshire).

Today, the Bethune home is under the purview of Bethune-Cookman University and is the jewel of the campus. Every day, visitors from around the world come to see the final resting place and home of Mary McLeod Bethune. Programs sponsored by the foundation for the local community include Bethune's birthday celebration, the Books and Bears reading program and Founder's Day events. The home also hosts local community members who come during family reunions, on sorority/fraternity outings and during B-CU's homecoming. During the school year, students visit the home to learn more about the founder's life, and prospective students also visit hoping to be inspired by the historic home. Students from Bethune-Cookman University serve as interns, giving tours just as they once did for Bethune's dedication ceremonies. Jada Wright-Greene was once a student intern in the foundation who was inspired by the home to go into the field of museum studies. Today, she is the owner of *Heritage Salon*, a magazine dedicated solely to the preservation and dissemination of the stories of African American museums:

> *Working at the Foundation allowed me the opportunity to fully embrace the love and the spirit of Dr. Bethune. I could not help being persistent and dedicated to my work because of that spirit and presence I felt when I was working in her home.*
>
> *My work eventually led me to start a blog and now a magazine,* Heritage Salon, *dedicated to African American museums, cultural institutions and historic homes and sites. Dr. Bethune's legacy, spirit and motivation led me to begin* Heritage Salon *Magazine which is the first and only publication dedicated to African American–focused institutions.*

Although Mrs. Bethune has gone on to be with God, her legacy continues to inspire generations through the Mary McLeod Bethune Foundation.

IN HER OWN WORDS

> *For the past two years, I have been formulating plans and ideas in my mind for the setting of what I term the Mary McLeod Bethune Foundation. The theme thought running through the whole idea is "not for myself but for others."*
>
> *The home where I live had been in the making for the past forty years. It seems now to have rounded out into a peaceful, spiritual, inspiring little corner where one might hide away for real meditation and backward looking and forward imagination.*
>
> *Little thoughts and ideas and trinkets have been gathered here from many corners of the earth. Citations and awards, unforgettable remembrances and treasures have come from here, there and everywhere. The walls have been covered with photographs of friends of many races and nations. The mottoes of inspiration and encouragement have found their way into our little center. Here the grass-covered lawn with shrubbery and flowers and*

beautiful trees add to the lustre [sic] *and uniqueness of the home. The roaring of the great ocean at night and by day lulls one to a dreamland of thinking and planning and dreaming.*

The nestling of the wonderful College buildings among the trees and the winding paths adjoining me: —the constant movement of fine young people from our America and many other countries; —the comfortable stillness beneath the moss-hung trees and the marvelous message from the pink azaleas in the garden—all give to a dreamer like me a sacredness that tells me to give fully and into this beautiful little sacred home, and its contents, and the soil upon which it stands to the Mary McLeod Bethune Foundation as a starter in the preservation of valuables and whatever personal affects [sic] *I may have of significance to the thousands that shall pass this way in the years to come.*

Here they will find inspiration. Those who are striving for the heights will find strength for their aspirations. The appraisers indicate that my gift can be counted in value to the amount of forty thousand dollars.

In my vision it seemed to me that this precious spot should not be selfishly claimed by my son and grandchildren. So another home is theirs and this I bequeath to boys and girls, to all races, creeds, classes and colors that they may find just a little of the inspiration and consecration that have come to me during these years of service.

The Foundation shall have a small board of trustees, a large number of a board of directors and a very large number of sponsors.

We want only men and women and boys and girls who believe in the rights and philosophies of Mary McLeod Bethune to participate in this great venture; those who will sponsor this venture with sincere determination and courage, in order that the little seed planted over 49 years ago may grow continually. Those who pass this way will surely be inspired and will realize that this which God has done for me, He will do also for you.

My friend Eleanor Roosevelt announced the launching. She was my houseguest for a night and a day with her charming companion Mrs. Malvina Thompson. It was gratifying to have our Mayor, the Honorable Tamm, our City Manager Harlow and members of city management with their various staffs—and citizens, white and black alike, to stand faithfully by during the launching of this Foundation.

They join the thousands of others who are showing their appreciation for the efforts of a loyal American citizen who has given her best to the cause of humanity. My files are being set up; my autobiography is being written; the home is becoming a shrine for posterity.

Part III

White Sands, Black Beaches

The Beginnings of Historic Bethune Beach

Florida is known for its sandy beaches and popular tourist destinations, including Miami, Key West and St. Augustine. What is least discussed is the history of the discriminatory practices of segregation that limited the access of African Americans throughout much of the twentieth century. One would think that beaches—a clear part of God's creation—would not be guarded by racism, but much like other public facilities, they were. In her quest to create space for African Americans to enjoy the same joys of the Sunshine State, Mary McLeod Bethune used her financial resources and influence to purchase her very own beach.

NEARBY CENTRAL AND NORTH FLORIDA BLACK BEACHES PROVIDE THE MODEL

Butler Beach was established in 1927 by Frank B. Butler and was one of the first black-owned beaches in Florida. The beach was located in St. Augustine between the Atlantic Ocean and the Matanzas River. Butler was a prominent and well-to-do African American who had been a successful grocery store owner and political activist. During its peak, the beach hosted African American guests, including Dr. Martin Luther King (who visited in 1964), and its amenities included picnic areas and playground facilities. Over a dozen black businesses thrived on the property, including Butler's Inn Hotel, and by the late 1940s, local African Americans had purchased investment properties. Butler Beach boasted a yearly Miss Butler Beach pageant, and holidays, especially Independence Day, hosted thousands of visitors.

American Beach was founded in 1935 just north of Jacksonville, Florida, on Amelia Island in Nassau County. The black-owned beach was started by Florida's first black millionaire, Abraham Lincoln Lewis, the successful businessman and founding president of the Afro-American Life Insurance Company based in Jacksonville. Advertising the beach as a place for "recreation and relaxation without humiliation," Lewis intended for it to protest Jim Crow conditions, which limited African American access to beaches. The company's Pension Bureau purchased the property, making special access to the property a part of the benefits package for employees. Company picnics were hosted for African American employees, and top sales agents were awarded with free stays in the beach's resort-style cabin properties. Lots were also available for $150, and many took advantage of the opportunity to own property in the prestigious area. The beach was open to local African Americans who came on bus trips from miles away, and each year thousands frequented the two-hundred-acre beach. Some of the most famous visitors included Mary McLeod Bethune, Cab Calloway, James Brown, Ray Charles and Zora Neale Hurston.

Paradise Park was designated as a "separate but equal" beach property for African Americans in Silver River in Ocala, Florida. Silver Spring Park owners Carl Ray and W.M. "Shorty" Davidson created the park in 1949 as an adjacent area to the whites-only Silver Spring Park. Known for its famous glass-bottomed boats, Silver Spring Park had attracted visitors since the late 1800s, yet it barred African Americans. With the creation of Paradise Park, large groups of African Americans came to swim on the beach, and churches would come to host baptisms and Easter egg hunts. The facility also had a dance floor, guided river tours, picnic areas, a gift shop and a restaurant—all run by an all-black staff (although owned by whites). From the park's opening in 1949 until 1967, Mr. Eddie Leroy Vereen managed it and promoted it in the local black community. During the Labor Day holiday, the highlight of the beach was its Miss Paradise Park pageant, which was hosted by the American Legion Post. In 1969, Paradise Park closed.

The Civil Rights Act of 1964 led to a sharp decrease in visitation to black beaches. The act ended segregation in public accommodations, and although it did not immediately integrate all of Florida's beaches, many became accessible. Over the years, African Americans who had previously driven many miles to reach the safe haven of black beaches found it easier to frequent desegregated beaches in their local areas. What was once the only place for people of color to enjoy the Atlantic Ocean became an afterthought throughout the black community. During the heyday of the black beaches, they were a place of cultural exchange and a needed escape from the hostile racial climate in Florida.

WORLD'S MOST FAMOUS BEACH

Daytona Beach was named after its founder, Matthias Day. Day was a wealthy businessman from Mansfield, Ohio, who sought an investment opportunity and purchased the land for $1,200 in 1870. In 1876, the town was incorporated. According to scholar Dr. Leonard R. Lempel, two of the twenty-six founding fathers of the town were African American: John Tolliver and Thaddeus S. Gooden. In 1889, railroad tycoon Henry Flagler purchased railways for what would become the Florida East Coast (FEC) Railway Company, extending rail service and making Daytona Beach more accessible to visitors. The building of railways also brought a number of workers into the area. In the early 1900s, the hard-packed, sandy beach became a popular place for car and motorcycle races, and it was soon deemed the "World's Most Famous Beach." As the popularity of the races grew and tourists came from all around to enjoy the beauty of the beach, Jim Crow reared his ugly head. By the 1920s, African Americans had been banned from the beaches, although they made up nearly half of the city's population by 1910.

By 1930, by law, African Americans were no longer permitted to use the boardwalks or public parks. In 1935, for a short time, there were two places made available during the summer and specific holidays that allowed African Americans restricted access to the beach. The two locations were Wilbur-by-the-Sea (located between present-day Daytona Beach Shores and Ponce Inlet) and a small space about five miles north of Ormond Beach. When black leaders decided to purchase a building at Wilbur-by-the-Sea to provide a changing area for visitors, locals burned the building to the ground. Albert McLeod Bethune, grandson of Mary Bethune, born in 1921, remembered being able to visit both locations as a child. In an interview, he stated, "When we got our experience with the use of the beach, it was through Mr. Gamble. He had a beach cottage, and every year on Easter Monday the family would allow Mrs. Bethune to bring her students for an all-day picnic." Albert McLeod Bethune Jr. spoke of how B-CC students enjoyed the opportunity to access the beach through Bethune's relationship with Mr. James Norris Gamble, the wealthy co-owner of Proctor and Gamble. In 1936, Mary attempted to galvanize black America to purchase beach property in Daytona Beach at Wilbur-by-the-Sea. In the *Chicago Defender*, a nationally distributed African American newspaper, she encouraged people to band together to buy the property. In the April 4, 1936 article "Mary McLeod Bethune Writes," she stated:

> *If we can get thinking, representative Negroes of this state and any other state to consider the advantages of a purchase of land on the great Atlantic Beach, in a short while we will be in possession of a wonderful residence and recreational district. It is necessary, however, to act speedily, for white people are working arduously to make the best of Florida's natural facilities in order to widely attract tourists and prospective residents. I am sure forward-looking Negroes everywhere will agree that this is a most unusual opportunity. Let us join hands and take advantage of it.*

Although she did not purchase the land, her vision to create a place for African Americans to enjoy the beaches of Florida would not die.

While the beaches of Daytona had become famous around the world and each year thousands flocked to see the popular races, African Americans were locked out of the experience. When B-CC hosted an African Students Union Convention in 1950 and attempted to take delegates to the beach, they were harassed by the city. The students had come from various American colleges representing their home countries of Nigeria, Ghana and Sierra Leone to discuss issues of colonialism in Africa, yet they faced similar conditions of oppression in Florida. As late as the 1960s, after the Civil Rights Act of 1964, which legally ended segregation in public facilities, African Americans were still subject to harassment on the beaches. In a 1998 interview for the *Orlando Sentinel*, local attorney Horace Hill recalled being questioned by police officers as he and a group of black ministers went to swim in the famed tourist area between the boardwalk and the band shell. According to the July 12, 1998 article, over thirty years after the incident, he still remembered the conversation as follows:

> *"Why are you all swimming here?" the officer asked. "Where do you suggest we swim?" Hill replied. The police officer scanned the horizon*

north and south. All he could see were white families frolicking in the sun. "Maybe somewhere down around the inlet," he said. In other words, miles away. "But that's not within the city limits of Daytona Beach," Hill said. "We pay taxes so that we can swim here." Flustered, the police officer backed off. "Well, go ahead and swim," he said. "Swim until you drown."

AMERICA'S NATURAL AIR-CONDITIONED YEAR-ROUND RESORT

After being in Daytona Beach for nearly four decades, experiencing limited access to the World's Most Famous Beach and not having her students be able to enjoy the luxury of the Atlantic Ocean at their leisure, Bethune decided it was time for change. She met with a few of Florida's wealthiest African American leaders and discussed the idea of purchasing a beach for the community. At the forefront of her mind was buying a beach where African Americans could enjoy the sun and ocean without shame or fear. Also, she thought the idea of ownership and selling shares to several African Americans would be an opportunity for economic empowerment. Bethune had known American Beach's owner A.L. Lewis for years and had stayed in the resort-style accommodations, but she felt it was time for her to bring the beach closer to home. She identified a two-and-a-half-mile strip of Volusia Beach and negotiated with its owner, Dana F. Fuquay. He was a very wealthy man who owned a large percentage of Volusia and Flagler Counties' intercostal land. She began the process of organizing a board and contacting possible investors.

On December 9, 1945, the board of directors met in Rogers Hotel in Tampa, Florida, and proceeded with the purchase of what would become Bethune-Volusia Beach by signing the charter. According to the meeting minutes, the officers, who had been determined before the meeting, were as follows: president, Mr. G.D. Rogers; executive vice-president, Mr. George W. Powell; vice-president, Dr. W.H. Gray; secretary, Mr. James A. Colston; and treasurer, Dr. Mary McLeod Bethune. Other persons to sign the charter included Professor J.N. Crooms, Mr. A.J. Smith, Dr. T.L. Lowrie, Attorney L.E. Thomas, Mr. A.C. Brinson, Dr. I.P. Davis and Dr. E.D. Strickland. The charter members were the who's who of black Florida. Among the group was G.D. Rogers, who had made his wealth as the founder of Tampa's Central Life Insurance Company, which he turned into a million-dollar business as president. J.N. Crooms was the principal and founder of Crooms Academy in Sanford, Florida, and James A. Colston was the second president of Bethune-Cookman University. Bethune had pulled together an impressive group of educators, lawyers and businessmen.

During the meeting, Attorney Thomas read a proposed constitution, and it was decided that the corporation would be capitalized at $25,000; the amount would need to be raised through the sale of 500 shares of common stock at a value of $50 per share. The total mortgage was $132,000, to be paid to Dana Fuquay. To begin the process, the board members purchased 228 shares of stock. Bethune, G.D. Rogers, James Colston, J.N. Crooms, George Powell and W.H. Gray all purchased 28 shares each, making up over half of the stocks purchased. The purchase could be made through cash, services or property. Executive committee members purchased 158 shares, and the remaining 114 were to be sold in cash only. The board also agreed to meet quarterly and that financial reports would be sent to its members. The group's organizational meeting was successful in laying the foundation for the sale of stock, and it gave board members the opportunity to financially commit to the success of the project. Although the board members and investors would change throughout the years, Bethune-Volusia Beach was officially established at the close of 1945.

INVESTMENT

When Bethune and her friends purchased Bethune-Volusia Beach, it was to provide not only access to the African American community but also an investment opportunity. Many of the lots today are worth millions of dollars, and for a person who might have paid a few hundred dollars for a lot in the 1940s, the return would be overwhelmingly profitable. During her life, Bethune always advocated for African Americans to own their own businesses—even her son, whom she helped to start a general store in the local community. She envisioned the beach properties as a way for people to make gains economically by obtaining a piece of Florida that had been kept from them for so long. Even in her last days, she called for African Americans to band together for economic empowerment. In her last will and testament, she stated:

> *I leave you the challenge of developing confidence in one another. As long as Negroes are hemmed into racial blocs by prejudice and pressure, it will be*

necessary for them to band together for economic betterment. Negro banks, insurance companies and other businesses are examples of successful racial economic enterprises. These institutions were made possible by vision and mutual aid. Confidence was vital in getting them started and keeping them going. Negroes have got to demonstrate still more confidence in each other in business. This kind of confidence will aid the economic rise of the race by bringing together the pennies and dollars of our people and ploughing them into useful channels. Economic separatism cannot be tolerated in this enlightened age, and it is not practicable. We must spread out as far and as fast as we can, but we must also help each other as we go.

The board immediately began to work on advertising the opportunity to purchase lots in black newspapers and created brochures highlighting features, including the beach's location, fishing options and cool weather. Salesmen were also sent out to speak at black churches and to various organizations. Bethune took a lead role in advertising through her weekly column in the *Chicago Defender*. She not only invested in the beach but also spent many birthdays and special holidays there to relax and enjoy the sun. Her columns reached thousands weekly and were distributed all over the nation through the *Defender*. She used this influence to encourage others to join those who had already purchased property on the beach. In her August 2, 1952 article, she wrote:

I have been dreaming this dream, now, for 34 years, and when I saw that crowd of 10,000 eager people pouring onto Bethune Beach last month. I was certain that the 800 families now owning property on our beach would soon be joined by hundreds of others. There is still room for another nine hundred owners; many who acquire property are acquiring several units, to provide additional space. I really believe that not only private owners but business men and women would find here the material for sound investment combined with great service. There is opportunity here for developing belief in ourselves and in demonstrating our own capabilities.

Advertised in brochures as "a playground controlled exclusively by our race," by 1947, lot sales at the beach were around $150,000, with fifty- by one-hundred-foot lots being sold for as low as $590 per lot. People from as far away as Philadelphia, Brooklyn, Montgomery and Charleston purchased property. In the next few years, there were many upgrades to the area, including the extension of water and power lines for those with plans to build homes. By 1951, Bethune Beach's president, G.D. Rogers, announced that over five hundred lots had been sold.

The popularity of the beach spread, and African Americans came by the thousands to Bethune-Volusia Beach, particularly on holidays and throughout the summer. During the July 4, 1950 holiday, over five thousand attendees came to the beach, according to lifeguards on duty. Visitors came from cities including Raleigh, North Carolina; New York; and Atlanta, while locals from Deland, Sanford and Jacksonville brought busloads of people. Over eight hundred students from B-CC also attended the July 4 festivities, while Bethune and the school's president, Dr. Richard V. Moore, also came for the day. According to newspaper accounts, the beach hosted a beauty contest and crowned Miss Mildred Jones (from Sanford, Florida) as the "Queen of Bethune Beach" for 1950. Contestants were selected at Bethune Beach and were crowned at the Coronation Ball held in Daytona Beach at the Cypress Street Recreation Center.

The local community hosted several events on the beach. On Easter Sunday, April 5, 1953, motorcycle races were held nearby featuring black top motorcycle racers Bill Gore, Milton Hall and Robert "Lead Belly" Brown. A ceremony was also held to honor Lawrence Silas. He was a successful cattle rancher who owned and operated a large ranch in Kissimmee, Florida. According to the author of *Black Florida*, scholar Kevin McCarthy, during the beach's early years, Lawrence Silas was instrumental in the establishment of Bethune-Volusia Beach, serving as a key investor. During the Easter celebration, it was declared to be "Mr. Silas Day," and he was given a citation for providing a model for successful business. During the festivities, he also exhibited a few of his best livestock. For those who participated in the events, it was a groundbreaking and historic occasion to see African Americans hosting celebrations on property owned solely by them. For many who lived in Florida, just miles away from beaches that barred them, it was inspiring to have a beautiful place to escape the ills of racism.

EXPANSION AND WELRICHA MOTEL

In 1951, plans began to build Welricha Motel on Bethune-Volusia Beach to offer patrons a resort-style vacation destination. Shares of Welricha Corporation stock were sold to raise capital to build the property. Mr. George Engram was largely responsible for the building of the motel. Engram had arrived in Daytona Beach in early 1933 after graduating from Tuskegee

Institute. When Bethune met him at Tuskegee, she encouraged him to move to Daytona Beach, where he later started his business, Engram Electric. She was instrumental in the success of the business, contracting most of her electrical projects with him for Bethune-Cookman College. Engram also taught in the Electrical Department at the college for many years. He became the vice-president of the board of directors and the general manager of Bethune-Volusia Beach and was very hands-on with the everyday oversight of the property. It was he who ensured that lifeguard services were provided through an agreement with the Volusia County Commission. When Welricha Motel was built, he became the secretary/treasurer while Mr. and Mrs. J.N. Crooms served as president and vice-president; together they were responsible for bringing the motel plans to fruition.

By the summer of 1952, the motel was up and running, with amenities including a recreation room and a dining room. Upon its final completion, Welricha featured fourteen units equipped with kitchenettes, refrigerators, tile bathrooms and full-sized bedrooms. The facilities were modern for the time and sold at rates from four to ten dollars per night or thirty to sixty dollars per week. For Bethune, the building of Welricha Motel was a dream fulfilled. After spending the July 4 holiday celebrating at the facility, she wrote, "On the Fourth of July, we sat here in this beautiful beach motel, which we have called 'Welricha' facing the waters of the great Atlantic Ocean, on the one side, and the north arm of the Indian River, on the other." Visitors were excited about the facilities and boasted about the first-class accommodations. One visitor wrote:

> The new Motel (like everything Mrs. Bethune does) is the last won in modern design—a half circle—and beauty. The room furnishings are lovely. The beach is becoming well known and now offers sufficient facilities to visitors. When the whole project is completed including dining hall, sun parlor, sun bath and auditorium, landscaping, streets, etc., it will be second to none in the nation for Negroes.

Brochures were made to invite potential visitors, highlighting the motel's "modern conveniences," including its bar and restaurant, Beach Casino. Advertisements featured beautiful girls, deemed "Bethune Beauties," from Bethune-Cookman College posed in their bathing suits around the Bethune-Volusia Beach entrance and in the motel. Great efforts were made to attract visitors, and the response was positive since it was one of the few places in Florida that featured such accommodations for African Americans.

CHALLENGES FOR BETHUNE-VOLUSIA BEACH

From the initial purchase of Bethune-Volusia Beach, board members knew that it would be a challenge, particularly since investors would need to be found quickly to expand the project. By 1952, while the beach was gaining popularity with visitors and the new motel was a hit, finances were shaky. In an effort to galvanize investors to become part of the historic venture, Bethune wrote a letter (which was published in African American newspapers) as a call to action:

> May I earnestly call upon you, the Negro Citizens of America—individuals and groups—to invest in this project in order that it may be held by and for Negroes? We have sent out a call to 10 outstanding Negro business men to invest $10,000 each in the project, take over the mortgage and approve further development, of the project, to enhance the sales program. We are soliciting and inviting your participation, through the purchase of Capital Stock at $50 a share. We are earnestly requesting the consideration of any Negro group or groups to take over the full mortgage on this valuable property, or to invest $5,000 or $10,000 on a mortgage basis. 860 lots have been sold and there are 1,600 left for sale, with a conservative sales value of $325,000.

In conclusion, she wrote:

> May I call upon the Churches, business and professional men and women, groups of all types—fraternal, business, social, civic—ordinary men and women of all walks of life, to pool their strength and help make this long, strong pull to keep the property in the possession of Negroes.
> I am writing this letter just after my 77th birthday. This is my last, long, earnest call for this type of endeavor. It is not a call for charity, but for an investment that will be of benefit to our own generation and our posterity. We are trying to build a resort that may be open to all people—not a segregated resort—one that is owned and controlled by Negro people. Will you answer my Call?

For Bethune, it was important to keep Bethune-Volusia Beach in the hands of the African American community, although it was open to all people. She saw the property as a place where a marginalized people could show the nation a model of racial cooperation. She intended to make the beach inclusive, unlike Daytona Beach, which had once barred her students and staff. Economically, she wanted it to be a place where African Americans could pool together their resources to have a shared space, a place that would exist in a time period when African Americans faced restrictions due to Jim Crow policies. When she made the call for assistance, the beach was flourishing in terms of popularity; however, it was struggling to stay afloat financially. According to the 1952 annual audit report, there were operating deficiencies, and more money was going out than coming in.

On May 18, 1955, Bethune-Volusia Beach lost its founder and Welricha Corporation lost its first vice-president when Mrs. Bethune passed away quietly in her home. From the very beginning, she had been an advocate for the expansion of the beach, and seeing her dream come to fruition was a lifelong goal fulfilled. For her, the beach was a safe haven where she spent birthdays, worked on her biography and watched her great-grandchildren play without the harsh realities of racism. Bethune used her influential position as a presidential advisor and women's club leader to promote Bethune-Volusia Beach, causing African Americans from around the nation to draw to it as investors and visitors. Her death was a striking blow to the place for which she had helped lay the foundations.

Over the next few years, Bethune-Volusia Beach continued to struggle, but in 1959, the stockholders came to a decision to obtain support from Volusia County. Several lots were deeded to the county with the agreement that it would build facilities—to include a pier, bathhouses, picnic areas and an auditorium—according to the late George Engram, treasurer and property manager during that time. For over two decades, the property sat without the promised accommodations being built. He fought for the city to return the property, but it never happened. Finally, in 1985, the city council agreed to allocate $34,000 toward the construction of the park, with the remaining $120,000 coming in from grants from the State Department of Natural Resources and the Ponce DeLeon Inlet Port Authority. In January 1986, the park was dedicated, and Engram was deemed honorary mayor.

With integration and the opportunity to visit beaches that had not previously been open to African Americans, Bethune-Volusia Beach began to lose its popularity. Many of the owners of the properties lived in states other than Florida, and the necessity of traveling to Florida was no longer there. Bethune's dream for the beach to remain in the hands of the African American community faded over time. Wealthy whites from the Orlando area begin to purchase properties, and many of the longtime investors who had bought lots for a few hundred dollars sold them for a few thousand.

Essentially, they made a profit, but many did not realize that the beach property was worth much more than what they had sold it for. It was very expensive to build houses since banks discriminated against black borrowers during segregation, and even afterward it was challenging, so the property was of no use to many who had bought it. Speculators bought empty lots at cheap prices and resold them for unimaginable profits. Many landowners experienced a hike in taxes and lost properties as a result of their inability to pay them.

George Engram became a key investor, buying many of the properties that people could not afford to keep. When interviewed for the *Orlando Sentinel* in 1985, he predicted, "I imagine in the next five or ten years you won't see a black down here at all." According to the census in the year of 2000, only 8 of the 742 inhabitants of the small community were black. What had been started with 100 percent black funds resulted in 1 percent black ownership at the turn of the twenty-first century, and the Engrams were one of the few families that managed to hold on to their property. In a 2003 interview with the *Orlando Sentinel*, Hester M. Bland, a longtime black resident dating back to the early 1970s, discussed the changing demographics of the beach. She remarked, "They came in and changed the whole complexion of the place...People look at you like you're a stranger." For years, she had witnessed the changing racial dynamic and now felt like an outsider in her own community. In fact, during the interview, while walking the beach, a young white man came out and asked, "What are you doing here?"

Today, Bethune-Volusia Beach is known as Bethune Beach, and many do not know the story of the woman whose name it bears. What was once a haven and place of financial investment for African Americans is now filled with million-dollar homes that are out of the financial reach of most Americans. Although Mary McLeod Bethune Park still stands with its basketball court, boardwalk and picnic areas, little is said about the courageous woman who galvanized black America to start its very own beach in the heart of New Smyrna Beach.

Part IV

A Mother, a Friend and a Boss Lady

The Inner Circle of Mrs. Bethune

Although Mrs. Bethune traveled around the world, served as a presidential consultant and is known by many as an international civil rights icon, to those who knew her best, she was a mother, a grandmother, a friend and a wonderful boss. In Daytona Beach, there are still many people who remember passing by, seeing her on the front porch or at Bethune-Cookman College (B-CC) football games. In the local community, she was and still is a humble yet revered hometown hero who touched the lives of many throughout the city.

"MY FONDEST MEMORIES OF MOTHER DEAR": MR. ALBERT BETHUNE JR.

Albert McLeod Bethune Jr. is the ninety-three-year-old grandson and legally adopted son of Mary McLeod Bethune. His father, Albert McLeod Bethune Sr., was born in 1899 and passed away at the age of ninety in 1989. Bethune Jr. was raised by his grandmother and has vivid memories of the times he shared with "Mother Dear," as he called her. Raised on the campus of B-CC from the time he was born in 1921, he later left as a young man to attend Morehouse College, where he received his bachelor's degree in Library Science in 1942. For thirty years he served as the chief circulation librarian at B-CC, and today he continues his dedication as the official historian for

Left: Mrs. Bethune and her beloved son Albert McLeod Bethune Sr. *courtesy of the Bethune-Cookman University Archives.*

Below: Albert Jr. and Albert Sr. in the 1950s. *Courtesy of the Bethune-Cookman University Archives.*

Holiday Greetings

BETHUNE MORTUARY

ALBERT BETHUNE   MARGARET BETHUNE   ALBERT BETHUNE, JR.

A Mother, a Friend and a Boss Lady

Mary Bethune, son Albert Sr., grandson Albert Jr. and great-grandkids during the early 1950s, gathered in the living room for family photos. *Courtesy of the Bethune-Cookman University Archives.*

the university. Although her son was grown (twenty-two years old) and living away from Daytona Beach in Miami in 1921, at the age of forty-six, Mary Bethune became a mother again.

> How did Mary Bethune, your grandmother, come to be your legal mother?
> *Some years* [ago] *when I was a little child, about five years old, she became my mother because my birth mother was Caucasian, and she came over to America and tried to get me from my grandmother, who was in charge of me. My father had brought me from Miami to Daytona Beach and turned me over to my grandmother. So to give my grandmother legal rights to me, she took it to the courts and adopted me as her legal son.*

Although he grew up without his biological mother in his daily life, Bethune Jr. expressed that he didn't feel slighted because his grandmother ensured that he was a happy child. Over the years, he was the center of her attention and even the center of B-CC's attention, as he was the school mascot for the sports teams as a child. Growing up on the campus,

81

everything that B-CC offered was at his disposal, including a nanny to look after him and to make sure that he was well taken care of.

> If you had to describe your grandmother (mother) in one word, what would it be?
> *Magnificent.*
> Can you elaborate?
> *Yes, she was a typical grandmother who bestowed on my father and myself all of the luxuries that it's humanly possible to give a child back in those days. She shared equally—everything she did for me, she did for him also. I'd say she was a magnificent grandmother, no holds barred. I think she spoiled both of us by being that magnificent mother.*

Growing up in the shadow of the nation's "First Lady of Negro America," Bethune Jr. admits that although Mary's fame was well known by many, he was unaware of just how powerful she was until years later. He also acknowledges that although she was an influential force in his life, he took his own path.

> What is your fondest memory of Mrs. Bethune?
> *My fondest memories of Mother Dear…there were so many that its hard for me to pick out one particular one because I've always said I was much older when I finally realized the importance of her work here in America with civil rights and other things. When I was growing up, I kind of strayed away from what she wanted out of me. And I never realized that she was the person she was until I was about thirty-five years old, when it really dawned on me what an outstanding, magnificent person she was.*
> Do you remember any advice she gave you?
> *She gave me advice all along my rearing process, but I did my thing the way I wanted to do. I didn't always accept her advice, and a lot of things I did wrong and a lot of things I did right, but I didn't let her control my journey to being an adult. I just followed the rules the way I wanted to follow. A lot of things I did she didn't know anything about. So that's the advice situation.*

Growing up in the Bethune household (known today as the Bethune Foundation) from 1921 onward, Bethune Jr. is the oldest living relative of Mary Bethune. B-CC was just 17 years old when he became a baby Wildcat, and he has witnessed the tremendous growth of the school firsthand as it approaches 111 years. His thirty-four years as the son of the school's founder gives him insight that few can provide.

What do you think she would want to be known for today?

The thing that I think she would want to be known for today is her international development of America because, you see, there were personally people who were around her—they considered her greatest accomplishments were Bethune-Cookman College and the National Council of Negro Women. Her greatest accomplishments done for America was with the National Youth Administration under President Roosevelt. She did a lot of things that enriched the lives of millions of people in America connected with the National Youth. Not Bethune-Cookman as it is today and not the National Council of Negro Women as it is today but the National Youth Administration and the position she held under the presidency of Franklin D. Roosevelt. That's her greatest accomplishment.

Is there anything that you would just like people to know about her?

Well she was the normal grandmother, Mother Dear. She wasn't—she had faults just like other individuals. I think sometimes we around the university try to put her on a pedestal of saintly hood. She was not a saint; she was a human being. She was just like any other. She had feelings. She had disappointments in her life, and I assume she had made mistakes in her life. So that was the way I see Mother Dear (as I call her), and she was lucky to be alive and live as long as she lived doing the things that she did during that time. Because a lot of the same people who came after her would have never made it by fascination or other methods. She was just lucky because she didn't fall in that class to have been fascinated by something because she followed her rules according to her law, which was legal, and some of it—like the segregation. She did not believe in segregation, and segregation was not practiced at Bethune-Cookman during her lifetime, under no circumstance, which was against the law in the state of Florida and in the country. So that's my remembrance of Mary McLeod Bethune.

"SHE WAS A FRIEND TO ME": MR. HAROLD V. LUCAS JR.

Known around campus as "Uncle Luke" to many, Harold V. Lucas Jr. has been a part of the Bethune-Cookman family since the 1930s. As the son of Harold V. Lucas Sr., he watched his father build B-CC's Business Administration program and accounting system as a professor and faculty member. His father was a graduate of New York University who came to

Harold Lucas and Mary Bethune during his tenure as a student. *Courtesy of the Bethune-Cookman University Archives.*

Daytona Beach to work with Mary Bethune. His memories of Bethune extend from frequenting the home with his father and growing up on the campus as a child. Mr. Lucas is also a 1953 graduate of B-CC and was a longtime track and football coach for the school.

I knew Mrs. Bethune as the president of Bethune-Cookman College at the time, but I knew her more intimately because of my, her relationship

Dedication

We proudly dedicate the 1953 B-Cean to the *Old Timers* of Bethune-Cookman College whose lives have become shining examples for us to follow—who have worked and are still working to help us and the College achieve our most cherished ambitions—whose lives may be simple ones, but whose services to mankind may bring great rewards—who have given unstintingly of their time and talent to help lay the foundation of our futures. One well known *Old Timer* is HAROLD V. LUCAS, SR., affectionately known to Bethune-Cookman grads throughout the U.S. as "Bro Luke." He is the first man to be employed by the College as a teacher. "Bro Luke" organized the Business Department here at the College, as well as that of Campbell High School. Through his wide experience and many talents he serves every department of the college. More students have trained under Mr. Lucas than under any other instructor at the college. We select "Bro Luke" not because he is the most outstanding *Old Timer*, for all of our *Old Timers* are outstanding, but we feel that because of his 32 years of unselfish service, his loyalty to this Institution and his love for all mankind, he is the example of the Spirit of the *Old Timers*, who have paved the way for those of us who work and study at Bethune-Cookman College.

Harold V. Lucas Sr. during his tenure at B-CC. *Courtesy of the Bethune-Cookman University Archives.*

with my father. My father was her man in waiting, you might say; he was her corresponding secretary at the time. He came down to establish an accounting system for Bethune-Cookman College at the time, and in doing so he fell into all of the other activities Mrs. Bethune wanted done. Like, he went down to Miami to check on a sundry shop that she had down there. Consequently, since my mother went to the hospital when I was seven and she died in the hospital, I used to have to go everywhere my dad went from the time I was seven until I left home. But I knew Mrs. Bethune as a very warm person. I know she was very businesslike, and I knew she was a person that had a vision, and if you were around her you would you would feel that vision because she would talk about what she wanted and how she wanted you to go about doing things and why you did things in a certain way. In her mind…I knew her as a person that, in her mind, KNEW what she wanted to do. The only thing she had to do, as I've told every president that has come here, is to buy into her dream. And if you bought into her dream, you got along with her; if you didn't buy into her dream, there were consequences because she was so set into doing things her way because she felt as though this was a vision from God. I knew her as a very religious person but also a very businesslike person. And a friend, she was a friend to me; her grandson said that she used to take more care of me than she did of him.

Watching Mrs. Bethune as a child and as a young adult, Lucas saw her through a changing yet consistent lens. Although Bethune was his father's boss, many times he was able to see his father's work at hand and how she managed B-CC and the activities of the school. For Lucas, B-CC was not just his father's job but also a home where he grew into a man. Although by the time Lucas was born, Bethune's status was well known throughout black America, he describes a woman who was concerned with small details that many people of her stature would have ignored.

When she was on the campus, what was it like? Was she the kind of boss who would be standoffish? Or was she into everything? *No she was into everything. In fact, my favorite example that I give to people of how concerned she was…If you were on the campus and she saw a piece of paper big enough for her to see, I don't care how far it was, she would say, "Dr. Robertson, see that piece of paper over there? Go over there and pick that piece of paper up for Mrs. Bethune because someone might be driving down Second Avenue and wanna give the school some money, and they'd use that as an excuse not to do it. 'See, I would give them some money, but look at all of that paper,'" and it would be one little piece of paper. So she was very precise, she was very concerned about every aspect of the—she always told the presidents, well, she always told the people and she passed that on to me, to tell the presidents when they come that you got to keep the campus pretty. You got to because that's the first thing people see. They say, "Where is Bethune-Cookman?" Well, it's over there somewhere.*

Well if you go over there and see it, when you first look at it, it's like an oasis because it's so pretty, and it's so well kept and that's the first view that you get of someone. The first impression, I guess you should say. "Well, at least they got a nice looking campus. I wonder what's inside?" When it was dirty outside, they would never get to the inside part. So she was concerned about how the campus looked and how the children acted when they went downtown. Uh, a lot of people say in the '50s they had to wear the blue and white; they didn't have to wear that downtown then. But it started off like that. You got ready to go downtown, and the girls used to have to wear the white blouses and, uh, and blue skirts. And the boys used to have to wear blue pants and shirts or something like that. Because she wanted them to know for their protection that they came under her umbrella; they were under her protection, and they also wanted to know if anything happened to one of those kids, they could say, well, that was a Bethune-Cookman kid, and they would inform us—not us but back at that time I was just a kid—but they would inform the people on campus, them in charge, that something happened to one of your kids. You know, it served as a two-edge sword; you know it was good for you and it bad for you. If you did something wrong, you got blamed, and if you did something right, she'd know who you were. And surprisingly, enough people would respect that because they respected her.

And one other thing about her: I never heard her raise her voice. I knew her from 1938 maybe to 1953, when I went into the service. I never heard her raise her voice. She didn't have to because the words that she would say would put you in your place or let you know how she felt about whatever it was. She'd say, "Well now, I know maybe we shouldn't do this"—it was sort of that melodic sort of voice. But she was always on point always.

When Mary McLeod Bethune passed away on May 18, 1955, the world responded to her death. Telegrams and sympathy cards were sent to her home from around the world, and thousands came to Daytona Beach to mourn her passing. At the age of twenty-three, Lucas had been impacted greatly by her and remembered vividly the passing of his friend.

I was in the army in Korea when she passed. Excuse me, I had gotten back from Korea, but I was in the army. Yeah, 1955; I got out the army in 1956.

Did you attend her funeral?

I was not able to get a pass.

Do you remember hearing that she passed away?

Oh yeah. Well, my daddy and Mrs. Bethune remained close throughout his lifetime. He died in 1956. And he sent me copies of all the newspaper things, all the newspaper articles saying that Mrs. Bethune had passed. He sent me a copy of the funeral program that they had. He sent everything that he could send during that time. I felt very sad because she was like a grandmother to me, because me being on the campus all the time and as close as I was to her. She had almost a triple role to me. Grandmother, college president, a boss in that she was my daddy's boss, so he respected her you know.

By the time Lucas met Bethune, she had formed the National Council of Negro Women; advised Presidents Coolidge, Hoover and Roosevelt; and established a successful college. Although she was older, her commitment to education and political activism was unwavering.

How would you describe Mrs. Bethune if you could use one word?

Dedicated. Whatever she was involved in, she was dedicated. League of Women, NAACP, B-CU, Mrs. Roosevelt—anything. I mean, if she took up the project, she was dedicated to it, and I don't think she spent much time doing things that she wasn't really interested in. And I think that's where a lot of people get so involved in so many things they cant give the thing that they need to, that they're most interested in, the credence that they should. But I would say she was dedicated, whatever it was she tasked or job or whatever, or responsibility that was placed on her, she was dedicated.

What were some of the sacrifices you felt she made for the school?

Well, she sacrificed her life. She put the school over everything else. She spent timeless amounts of time away from the school in order to try to better the school. She was a visionary…she had, as I mentioned before, she kind of knew what she wanted and she knew what it was gonna take to do it. And there was no sub—as my coach would say, "There was no substitute for work" for her. However many hours…I know my dad used to stay here to ten, eleven o'clock at night; that's why I used to go upstairs. They would say, "Well, we not through yet; just go up there in my bed and lay down until we get through." But if it fit into her dream, it became your dream because she was just that influential. And you could see…if you were concerned about it, you could see where she was trying to go. And you could see the obstacles that might be in front of her but how she would weave that little web to pull all of that stuff in. You know. The rich men or the people that sing or the people like Mrs. Hacker; they used to have the chorus that we had—or concert choral, it was finally called—they used to go all over the world singing. And she felt that people like to hear black people sing, and they start off with Negro spirituals and hymns and all that and then it advanced to the Italian street song. People used to come from across the river to see the black lady known as Virginia Fulworth singing the Italian street song. That was like in '46 or '44, '45, '46—back in there when we had communion. She was always looking for that little thing to bring people to Bethune. In turn, that meant that she had to do a lot of going herself 'cause she had to sell her product. You didn't have TV and all that stuff back like they got. Facebook, and Twitter…witter, or whatever it is. They didn't have all of that stuff back then. So it was a personal contact, and she was very keen in making good contacts like Eleanor Roosevelt. You know she was responsible for getting up WPA programs, which were the work programs down here. She met Mr. Gamble and Mr. Rockefeller and all those guys…she was able to convince them, and she'd sell pies and give pies or whatever; the potato pies were no joke. That's one of the ways that we started. We—well, I say we 'cause it seem like I been around here so long.

In 1923, during the merger of the Bethune's all-girls school with Cookman Institute, she began to make accommodations for male students. In that same year, the football team was organized, and throughout the next few years, basketball, tennis and soccer were added. As a child, Lucas was the school mascot, taking the place of Albert McLeod Bethune Jr. once he became a bit older.

What's your fondest memory of Mrs. Bethune?
Seeing her enjoy athletics. She used to love the football team. And when—see, I've always been close to the football team—and when they would say that she was coming down to watch the guys practice, even when I was a little kid, before I played and all that stuff, when she would come down and watch the guys practice and tell them, say, "You all got to be strong out there! You got to get in shape! You got to learn your plays! You got to do all of that stuff 'cause if you can learn this, you can learn your academic stuff. How can you know all them plays and not know your academics? No." So there has to be some carryover in both ways. But everybody used to love to see her come down. She'd be in her car, you know; she'd drive down where the band field is over there. It was a garden like down there back in those days. And she'd come down there and watch the guys practice for a little bit. See, she was all around the campus; she just didn't sit up in her office. You

know—and say, "What's going on over there?" See, I used to see her down in the vocation shop when we had…where they used to teach carpentry and brick masonry and all of that stuff. She'd go down there to see how things were going in addition to all of the traveling that she did for the school. So my fondest memory is just seeing her walk around the campus. Every time I would see her walking around campus, especially if I wasn't at school— you know, before I got to go to Bethune or whatever—I'd just walk around with her, you know. That's how we happened to be down there that day when she took the picture just walking around looking at things.

During the time that Bethune lived in Florida, she created an atmosphere in Daytona Beach where African Americans, although segregated, had their own space to flourish as business owners, leaders and educators. Many, including influential theologian Howard Thurman, have said that the presence of her school gave hope to black Daytona. In 1946, when Jackie Robinson came to Florida for spring training with the Montreal Royals, he was threatened in Sanford and was able to find refuge in Daytona Beach. After being denied the right to play in Jacksonville, Deland and Sanford, Robinson found that Daytona Beach was the only town where he could play. He played the historic game at City Island Baseball Park, which has since been renamed Jackie Robinson Ballpark in his honor. Bethune's influence in Daytona Beach was a clear factor in his ability to play in the history-making game and his journey toward Major League Baseball.

What do you feel was Mary Bethune's greatest achievement here in Florida?
The development of Bethune to me, and unseen things where the atmosphere (I guess that's a word I can use) that she developed in the city of Daytona that reached far out. Because, you see, she would get people from Miami, and she had a little place down in Miami (as I fore mentioned), and West Palm Beach and all of those places knew of Mrs. Bethune and that's why they wanted to come to school. Well, she had to have had some influence on them for them to come to school. But she just…she was like a spider; she just put that web out there and just got you. And if she got you, she got you.
Here's a question that I hadn't thought about before now: were you here when Jackie Robinson played? Because you talked about the atmosphere that Mrs. Bethune created. A lot of people say that it was the atmosphere that she'd created in Daytona Beach that allowed him to be able to play.

JACKIE ROBINSON

MOLLIE GOLDBURG

Outstanding Visitors

DR. RALPH BUNCHE

DR. AND MRS. McKINLEY, MISS KRASHMA
DR. WILLIAMS, DR. MOORE

Jackie Robinson receiving his honorary degree from B-CC and Ralph Bunche speaking during commencement in 1954. *Courtesy of the Bethune-Cookman University Archives.*

When Jackie Robinson came here, I was in the ninth grade. He spoke at our high school. I was, like I said, in the ninth grade in junior high getting ready to go into senior high. He came here, and he stayed with Mrs. Duff Harris, who was a reporter for the Westside News, the news for colored people in the News Journal. That's who he stayed with. She had, as I mentioned, she had created an atmosphere here that was—I won't say controlled, but this campus was controlled. And the people respected what went on here as something that was good. OK? So when Mrs. Bethune wrapped her arms around Jackie Robinson and, of all the people, Sam Jones, Roy Campanella and all of those that came here, the community, realizing that they had something that was new, being the integration thing, they sort of leaned on Bethune to help with any problems that they might have. So… but the atmosphere was not like it was in other parts of the country. In other words, here I think you got a little benefit of the doubt that everything's gonna be all right, but if it wasn't all right, there were people in place that were gone see that things got straightened out. There was black people and white people. White people that like Mrs. Bethune and black people that liked Mrs. Bethune, and it was, you know, sort of a—Bethune, the atmosphere that Bethune had set prior to that sort of lended [sic] toward the openness, and she had a lot of community leaders and stuff, you know, not in her pocket, but she had their ears. See, a lot of times you don't have to get money from people, but if you got their ear, they can tell you, "Well, I can't help you but don't let them do this" or they can help her do this. See what I'm saying? So, when Jackie Robinson came here, we used to go out; I used to go out there on the field, out there where the building is out there close to Nova Road now. I forgot what they call it. But that's where they used to practice when they first came here. It was called Kelly Field back in the day, and we used to go out there and shag balls for him, and you know, he was very friendly. He would talk to you and a lot of other guys…now, Jackie Robinson lived with Mrs. Dufferin Harris, but there was a place called Littleton's Tourist Court; that's where a lot of those other guys used to live. That was out there on South Campbell Street or South Martin Luther King, out there. Like they used to call, little places where black chauffeurs and all that used to live. You know, they had white people on the other side, and they would stay over there on their side. It was called a Tourist Court. It was Littleton's Tourist Court.

What do you think she would want to be known for today?
As an initiator. A person that planted a seed and did her damnedest to make sure that it grew like it was suppose to grow.

Today, Bethune-Cookman University's College of Entrepreneurship and Business boasts degrees in accounting, finance and hospitality management, just to name a few. In the earlier years, Harold V. Lucas Sr. was instrumental in working with Bethune to solidify the Business Administration Department, but interestingly enough, he almost started his own mini business school under Bethune's instruction.

Is there anything that you just want people to know about Mrs. Bethune or any words that you just want to share?

You know, it sounds cliché, but she was a firm but fair person. And I don't mean as long as you do as I say do—you know. She had enough sense to look back and say, "Well, maybe we can try that." You know—she was an innovator. She was a—she was a visionary. She knew what she wanted to do, she knew how to do what she wanted to do…all that she wanted you to do was listen to her. If you listened to her, she was gonna convince you that Bethune-Cookman was gonna be the place to be. Bethune-Cookman was gonna set itself apart from a lot of the other things that might come. That's why we been able to be here so long…because we are different, we are caring. Mrs. Bethune would give you the axe now, don't misunderstand me. She told my daddy if you don't bring those students that you got down there at your house, that you're teaching, to the campus, you're gonna get fired. That's the part I didn't even mention.

You can go back to that.

OK. Well, my dad being a Yankee from Brooklyn and being an entrepreneur, having an entrepreneurial spirit, he said he did whatever Mrs. Bethune wanted, but in 1923, he built a house right down there on Jefferson Street. It was right next to the house I live in now, and its still there. And downstairs in that house he had a little classroom, and he had a little print shop where he used to teach people for twenty-five cents a week how to type. He had a little print shop where he used to run up all the church bulletins and stuff, all the little handbills and stuff for the grocery stores, and he used to do all the handbills. And my mother, before she got sick, they used to go around all and do that stuff with all the handbills and the church bulletins and all. And so he had about twelve to fifteen people from the community that wanted to learn how to type. Now, he bought some old typewriters from a guy named Mr. English, who was down there on Ivy Lane. And when the business department started, Bethune used to use his typewriters because he was teaching here and doing work here in the morning and at Campbell Street in the afternoon (which was a high school). So she noticed all these people that were taking typing and all, and she told him, and I have this—did I show it to you? In the contract, where it said that you need to bring the people up here? Yeah, because she referred to the Accounting Department as the Business Department because you need to bring those people up here because they can do the typing, they can learn how to type. That's how the Business Department got started. He brought the kids that he was—of course, at that time, you know, this was a junior high school, you know a high school as well as a—so he brought the kids up here and taught them, and they entered school here and they learned how to type and went to Bethune.

So that means his business had to stop?

Yeah. He just shifted gears and started encouraging kids to come, and that's how the Business Department got started. He didn't have time to do that stuff down there at the house, but he (again) kept his job and an increase in salary. You see, back in the old days, you learned that a little bit of something is better than a whole lot of nothing. So he might have lost some twenty-five-cent students, but the school got a Business Department, and they were able to develop that.

From the time that Lucas was about five years old (1937) until now (2015), he has been part of the Bethune-Cookman community; for him, it is much more than a school but also a major contributor to his development as a person.

Mary Bethune and Duke Ellington during the 1950s on the campus of B-CC. *Courtesy of the Bethune-Cookman University Archives.*

What has Bethune-Cookman College meant to you?

I could sit here and tell you in one word or I could sit here and talk to you all night. Bethune-Cookman College has meant everything to me. If it were not for Bethune-Cookman and New Mount Zion Baptist Church—I've been a member there since before I was here…since I was three years old. Here, I was at least five before I got involved. But Bethune-Cookman gave me determination to do a job—complete a job. It gave me compassion to realize that everything is not equal; you're gonna run into hard times. It's not—as a coach for over fifty years, my thing was—and it's not what happened to you; it's how you respond to what happened to you. Because my dad was handicapped…that's always been very important to me. Because even though he was handicapped, he still did a lot of good stuff.

"I was considered a protégé of hers": Dr. Cleo Higgins

Dr. Cleo Mildred Surry McCray Higgins is a ninety-one-year-old former faculty member of Bethune-Cookman College, where she served for twenty-nine years. During her tenure, she had the pleasure of working with Mary McLeod Bethune when Bethune served as university president from 1946 to 1947. In later years, she rose to the position of dean of faculty and vice-president of academic affairs under the presidency of Dr. Oswald Bronson. During her tenure, she developed the official seal for B-CC, which is still used today with modifications. She was also the tenth national president of Sigma Gamma Sorority Inc., an organization of which she has been a member for over seventy years. As a member of the faculty of B-CC and someone who was drawn to the school because of Bethune's presence, Higgins's memories are a testament to Bethune's powerful leadership abilities.

Dr. Higgins, please tell me how you knew Mrs. Bethune and what was your relationship with her?

I met Mrs. Bethune in the fall of 1943; the late fall on the campus of Bethune-Cookman College. I had been sent to the state of Florida by my alma mater, Lemoyne College in Memphis, Tennessee, to do my practice teaching in that, my senior year, '43–'44, at Fessenden Academy, which was a school for black boys near Ocala. While there, having arrived there in the late fall, October '43, actually, I was the English teacher and the

SPONSOR

Miss Cleo M. Surry

Cleo Surry (Higgins). *Courtesy of the Bethune-Cookman University Archives.*

senior student doing an internship. The girls' basketball coach left Fessenden Academy for some reason, and I was asked to take the team to coach because I had played basketball at Lemoyne (my college). And so I did. In the course of that semester, Fessenden Academy and West Palm Beach (I think it was West Palm Beach) [were] scheduled to meet in basketball (boys' and girls' teams). They found I'd like to be the coach for the girls, and we met and played—can't think of the name of the school right now. The court at Bethune-Cookman and bringing athletic teams to the campus was a way of recruiting. We met the two schools... teams met and played on the basketball court, which was located—it was the ground, it made a court—at the north end of the back of White Hall. That's where the basketball court was. That was my reason for coming, bringing a group of young people from the academy to Daytona Beach.

As I pulled up on the campus, entering the gate to the east, and I stopped my car right in front of the east far side of White Hall. There was there, at that time, a tree—a beautiful tree, which was called the Queen Mary Tree. And we got out of the car, and I remember that I was standing there looking at that tree and the beautiful campus because it was so clean. It was a beautiful sunshiny day, and I heard a voice coming up on my left as it was saying, "Hello, my dear," and when I turned around, that happened to be Mrs. Bethune. And she had—I never forget—she was wearing...either it was a white or gray sweater and, of course, it was October. What we jokingly called thereafter those Bethune shoes—they were Oxford shoes with a seemingly long toe that was squared at the end of the shoe, not a pointed toe but a squared toe. And when I heard this voice that said, "Hello, my dear," and when I turned around, it was Mrs. Bethune wearing those shoes, as I recall, a dark skirt but definitely a white or light gray heavy sweater; it was cool in October at that time. And she said, "Hello, my dear," and I was just all stricken because I knew that that was Mrs. Bethune. I had been a graduate of—I was a graduate of Dusable High School in Chicago, and I knew of her work there. And she lived—she visited the Masons, M.C.B. Mason, my future husband's grandfather that I just mentioned to you before, whenever she came to Chicago. But I had never met her; in fact, I knew Billy (my—who was the grandson of M.C.B. Mason) but I didn't know anything about the connect with Mrs. Bethune—you know, family connections. So from that point on, I always remembered her greeting me: "Hello, my dear." We played, and I don't remember who won or lost, but it was a very pleasant visit. The school that we played was Roosevelt High School out of West Palm Beach, Florida. Fessenden Academy met and played them when I was the girls' basketball coach; boys' and girls' teams played.

Upon finishing college and her student teaching, Higgins was drawn to Florida, but due to segregation she wasn't able to attend the school she thought she should attend. Although she is now in her nineties, the memories of rejection are still present, but she also remembers the joy of working with a civil rights legend and educator. For her, Bethune filled a void in the state of Florida, one that almost left her without the opportunity to make the state her new home.

I was to march to finish my baccalaureate work that June, and I did, and I thought I would like to stay in Florida. I liked what I had seen and so forth. So I applied to the University of Florida and was I was thereupon dismayed to receive a letter from them saying…from the university saying we don't admit Negroes; we'll give you $200 to attend any school you'd like—any university you'd like to. I kept that letter until I realized what it was doing to me and how it was making me feel. I considered the University of Florida an antagonist for various reasons so I burned it. I remember burning and putting a match to it. As I took the…after I took the degree (Lemoyne's degree), I was valedictorian, and Bethune-Cookman offered me a job. I could have come to Bethune-Cookman or—and I had an offer from Alabama State. Seems I had another offer from somewhere. Anyway, Alabama State paid more than Bethune-Cookman, but I wanted to come back—I wanted to come to Bethune-Cookman because that's where Dr. Mary McLeod Bethune was. That's why I came and started work here September of '45 after…uh, uh, that was '44…I went to graduate school '44 to '45, then I came to work for Bethune-Cookman [in the] fall of 1945 for much less than what Alabama State would have paid or had offered to pay me. I worked the year '45 to '46 under the then president

Colston—doctor, I think he was—James A. Colston and his wife (can't think of her name). Anyway, then at the…at the end of that first year, Mrs. Bethune, Colston left, and Mrs. Bethune resumed her presidency [in] *'46–'47 and she was my president, and she was in and out and around and about the campus doing all of her great works, meetings and et cetera.*

As a young professional, Higgins became a mentee of Bethune's, and she received valuable lessons as an employee of B-CC. She was dependable, hardworking and a valuable asset to the school. Bethune would not forget all that she did for her.

I know one of the first things I remember…she said to me (which I was so happy about), I was considered a protégé of hers, and the National Council of Negro Women under Dr. Dorothy Height came to recognize that, and they promoted me as that. She—I wanted to go to graduate school, and I wanted to go on and get my doctorate, and I remember Mrs. Bethune told the…she just told the bishop, and I guess the Florida State Conference…anyway, the United Methodist in the state of Florida: "Give Cleo a fellowship. She wants to go to school." And they did. And that was one of several; I never paid tuition, and it was followed by Gutenheim, then I had a Ford, then I had a Rockefeller and something else. Anyway, I had all these fellowships, and it helped through school. And she was very happy about me for several reasons, and she told me that one reason she liked me was I liked to work! [In her Mary Bethune voice,] *"You like to work and that's what you're here for." Through the years, I knew her, and I had materials and programs and so forth. I kept up with her, though she was on and off campus and I was on and off campus during those years when I was gone attending graduate school somewhere. But it was the spring of '55—April, in fact—Easter Sunday that I married Billy Higgins, Mame Mason Higgins's grandson—not grandson, his mother. And that was Easter Sunday, and Mrs. Bethune gave us our wedding breakfast. I did have…I didn't ever take pictures at that breakfast. I've always regretted that. Because we married at Stewart Memorial and Reverend, he married us in the parsonage Easter Sunday morning. And that was 1955. I went back to school—went back to Wisconsin—and I had been there for maybe a week going on two weeks, I think, when she died. I couldn't get back to the funeral, but what's his name? Reverend…?*
Murray—oh, Thurman.
Reverend Thurman did the eulogy, and I have a copy of it. I prize that copy and, as I said, that picture that I have of him, Mrs. Bethune and Sue Bailey sitting on the couch in her study.

Many times, Bethune was away traveling and raising money for the school, and her staff/faculty had to be trustworthy and independent of her day-to-day management. With B-CC consistently growing, she was very selective about whom she chose to work with her precious jewel.

When you worked with Mrs. Bethune in 1946, what kind of boss was she?

Boss?

Yes.

She wasn't one who stood over you. As…she had expectations of [in her Mary Bethune voice] *"those who worked at Bethune Cookman." And I remember—can't think of the particular incident, but I recall these words the other day. Maybe the situation will recur in my memory, but I remember there were some remarks in this incident about the work and the load of work or something. I remember Mrs. Bethune saying* [in her Mary Bethune voice], *"Yes, but that's why you came here. That's the reason for your being here." In other words, that was a very impressive moment for me because she expected work. You play and you laugh—oh boy, she had a laugh, and she liked to laugh, but she also* [in her Mary Bethune voice] *"believed in work." And she wanted to know* [in her Mary Bethune voice] *"what was going on on campus," and if she didn't hear anything, she would ask us, "What's going on?" She had a great sense of humor. Did I answer your question?*

During that year that you worked for Mrs. Bethune, what was your position at Bethune-Cookman?

The English teacher. And she was proud of me because, well, I had just come out of graduate school from UW–Wisconsin, and I liked to work. And she…I remember her saying that "I'm so glad you're here because we do not now have to report to the state department." There before, I'm not sure what the relationship was or how the rating—what is it? Southern Association had it set up, but the English—in fact, I can't remember—that if all the departments of Bethune-Cookman had to be approved by SIC or not, but I know that the…I distinctly remember Mrs. Bethune saying that she was so happy that the "English department, now we've got an English professor, an English teacher, and we do not have to, Bethune Cookman does not have to report to the state department." It will be approved by the state. I remember that. So she was pleased with that. And I remember also another thing that was just delightful for me. She was a great speaker herself. She could speak extemporaneously on anything that she wanted to talk about, and she could do so at length. She could

*go at length. We knew that when she came to campus, this was '46–'47, that
there would be an assembly, and everybody would go to chapel in White Hall
because she was going to speak. And she did. She would tell us where she'd
been and what she'd done, and there was no scrounging or sighing or ruffling,
but the word would get around: "Mrs. Bethune is back. Mrs. Bethune is on
campus." So everyone knew there would be an assembly because she would tell
us what she would be doing and what was happening and so forth…and her
travels and so forth and so forth.*

In remembering the years she spent at B-CC, even after Bethune's
passing, Higgins remembers that it was the spirit of the great founder and
her foundation that kept the school progressing forward.

*We didn't have to pump up morale. You see, she was here. She was—she
was alive among us, and I think that just permeated life on the campus
and the curriculum and just life among the inhabitants of this planet of
Bethune-Cookman.*

*We were a part of her, and she [was] a part of us, and she let you know
that you were here to work. We didn't have janitors and yard men to keep
the placed picked up when she was the president—we picked…the students
picked up, and if the place became too much trash or paper or whatever
collected then just call; we'll just stop and clean up the campus. That was
before we had maintenance crew. That was Mrs. Bethune.*

"…THE STORY OF THE LAST DAY THAT SHE WAS ALIVE": MRS. SENORITA LOCKLEAR

Ms. Senorita Locklear was Bethune's last secretary and a longtime employee
for years after her 1955 death. Her memories of Bethune's last few months
and even the last day that she was alive give her a story that is unique
and personal. Many times, she was there when no one else was and saw
Bethune's sick days, her joyful moments and the power she had to capture
the attention of those who visited the Mary McLeod Bethune Foundation.

How did you know Mrs. Bethune?
*Well, I served as her personal/business secretary for eleven months and
two weeks. I began my tenure with her on June 1, 1954; she passed away*

on May 18, 1955. Had she lived until then, I would have completed twelve wonderful months that I will always treasure.

If you could describe Mrs. Bethune using one word, what would it be?

Determined—she was determined, she was focused and if she had her mind on it, she was determined to see it through to fruition. I guess the one word was determined.

SENORITA W. CRAWFORD
Secretary to the Business Manager

Senorita Crawford (Locklear). *Courtesy of the Bethune-Cookman University Archives.*

Shortly before Locklear arrived, Bethune had started the Bethune Foundation, which operated out of her home. Although she had retired from most of her organizations and as B-CC's president, she continued to work everyday and had many projects that were still in the works when she passed away. The foundation was her home, but it was the office and workplace for Locklear. Over time, as Bethune retreated into her home, visitors came, just as they do today, to meet the legend. Since Daytona Beach was segregated, allowing only whites to enjoy the beach, many of those who came there for vacation were not African American.

What was a typical day? I mean, tell us about a typical day in the foundation.

Well, a typical day in the foundation…it's a really, well, number one, she came downstairs to the office to her desk, and we always started the day whenever she came down, reading from The Upper Room. She would read one day, I would read the next day, and then she would begin her duties. She…with this being tourists' town, visitors were constantly coming there. Oh, I shouldn't say—well, I'm gonna say it because this is a fact—whites…some came to renew their acquaintance; others came to meet her for the first time, but in comparing the number of blacks to the number of whites, 75 percent of the people who came were white. We didn't recognize her, you know, during that time. I guess whatever is in your own doorstep…you don't really know the importance of it. But the whites were constantly there.

I'll give you an example: one day, the doorbell rang. It was about four o'clock, and I answered it, and it was this white there with her little girl who was about four. She was from Minnesota, I believe, and she said, "My name is (I don't remember)"—it's in the guest book, and that's one thing I want to talk about. And she said, "We're visiting Daytona Beach, and I just want my little girl to say that she had the privilege of meeting Mrs. Bethune." Now, that's the recognition that the whites gave her. So I told her that Mrs. Bethune was having her dinner, and I brought her in to the office and she was seated. So I went into the dining room and I said, "Mrs. Bethune Mrs. (whatever her name was, I can't remember her name...it's here), and she has her little girl and she just wants her little girl to say she had the privilege of meeting you when she grows up." So Mrs. Bethune says, "Don't have them waiting...show them into the dining room."

So we went into the dining room, and just as we got from the living room to walk from the living room to walk into the dining room, Mrs. Bethune sat at the head of the table. She only had one meal in the dining room, and that was her dinner. Her breakfast and lunch she had there. But she was sitting at the head of the table, and as we entered (I just have to show you this), as we entered, when we got to the dining room, the lady said, "Go up and meet Mrs. Bethune." She was prodding her, and the little girl was backing up...you know, she didn't wanna go. She said, "Go up." Mrs. Bethune put her silver down, and she said, "Come here, my little angel." And that girl, that little girl, she walked just as if she were hypnotized. All she—now, that's what her presence meant to a four-year-old. And I told her I wish that I had had a camera to take a picture before, with her mother prodding her and she was backing up, and Mrs. Bethune doing this. That was the most beautiful thing you would wanna see, and she walked straight into her arms. But that was one of the most impressive ones. They would come, and Mrs. Bethune would have them, and they would talk and they would ask her questions and she delighted in that. You could see the difference...her eyes told a story. If you looked at her eyes, all she had to do was look at you; it was just like a magnet. Well, that was the day, then she would do her dictations; she would look at them, then do the dictation. Well, that was the day and...let me see what can I say.

Although she spent a lot of time away from home in the earlier years and gave a lot of her energy to various causes, Bethune loved family time. Although she gave birth to one son, her family had grown tremendously with his family and her grandson's family. She often surrounded herself with her grandkids, and she was proud to have such a beautiful family.

Mary Bethune spending family time with great-grandkids Donald and Patricia Bethune in her home. *Courtesy of the Bethune-Cookman University Archives.*

When her grandchildren—this is what I want to say—Mrs. Bethune was family oriented (I'm talking from the personal side). She was family oriented. She loved her family, her son, her grandson (who has a dual role—you know that) and the three grands that were there. When they would come over after school in the afternoon, the minute Nicky, Sammy, Pat—and when they would walk in, her eyes would just light up. And she would…two would be sitting on this knee and one would be sitting here, and she just loved them and it made a difference. Because sometimes she would be sort of down, but if those kids came in there, it was a whole—and some days, you know, she wasn't feeling well, and she would be upstairs in her bedroom. They came in and they would go up those stairs to see her, and it made all the difference in the world. She loved her family. That's about all I can say about the day.

Three Requests on the Last Day

On the last day that she was alive, Mary was not sick or down and seemed to be her normal self, but she did make three very unusual requests. At the time, Senorita didn't find any of the requests unusual, but in hindsight, she feels that Mary must have felt that she needed to get things in order.

But I want to tell you, you know the story of the last day that she was alive, May 18?

I know some of it, but I would like it if you would like to talk about it.

When she came downstairs, and after we had read from The Upper Room, she asked…she said, "Senorita, how many chapters has Rackham Holt completed?" Rackham Holt was there at the time doing the biography. Rackham Holt lived in Ranslow. What she would do was, she would come over every day, interview Mrs. Bethune, then she would go back to Ranslow. And some weekends, they would spend the weekend at Bethune-Volusia Beach because there would be no interruptions (and they can do stuff). So between the office and Bethune-Volusia Beach, Rackham would interview her, and when she would complete a chapter, she would bring it over for Mrs. Bethune to read. Mrs. Bethune would edit it; after she would edit it, Rackham Holt would go back to Ranslow and print it in the final copy. I mean, type it because back at that time, you know in '55, it was typing, and it was done in three copies. The original was sent to Double Day, Rackham Holt kept a copy and Mrs. Bethune kept a copy. So that day—well, let me back up. When I first came on my first day, she was telling me about the office and the procedures, and she told me what was in the safe and that's one thing. She had a safe there in the office, and that's where all of her important documents were kept. So that day, she pointed out three things there: her will; the chapters (these are things that were kept in the safe), the chapters that Rackham Holt had done; and her business affairs. Those three things, those were the most—she stressed the importance of those, and they were kept under lock in the safe. They were never out at all. So she was telling me the contents of the safe and what was most important to her, and those are three. Now, on May 18, when she came down that morning after we had our devotion, the question she asked me was: "Senorita, how many chapters has Rackham completed on my life?" And I told her. So she said, "Will you get them out for me?" And I said sure. I got them out, and she said, "Will you read them to me?" So I said, remember Mrs. Bethune, each chapter is read to you before it's sent to Double Day. She said, "Yes, but I hear it in bits and pieces. I hear one chapter today and it'll be three or four weeks and I'll hear another chapter." She said, "But I want to hear it all together." So I started reading, and she was sitting in her chair with her eyes closed just taking it all in when…and when I was reading, Mary Divers, Ms. Divers, came over. Mrs. Bethune—you heard of, you know about Mrs. Divers, right?

No, ma'am.

Oh! She was—Mrs. Bethune was her mentor. She met Mrs. Bethune when she was in graduate school in Atlanta University getting her master's, and Mrs. Bethune came to speak at Atlanta University. She met her and there was a bond, and she was one of the two persons, she and Mr. Rod, came to see her every day. You know about Mr. Rodriguez?

Edward Rodriguez was Mrs. Bethune's foster son. When he met Bethune in his teen years, he revealed that he was an orphan, and she brought him to Daytona to put him in school. Over the years, Rodriguez repaid her with his loyalty and dedication to her, the foundation and B-CC.

Well, those two, now they…I can say they came more than her family did. Really, every day they came over. "Mrs. Bethune, how are you?" So Ms. Divers came in while I was reading; her name was Mary, so Mrs. Bethune said, "Mary, how many chapters?" I mean, excuse me…"Do you have any more classes? When is your next class?" She said, "I don't have a class until this afternoon, Mrs. Bethune." She said, "Well, I tell you—would you do something for me?" She said, "Senorita is reading the chapters that Rackham has completed, but she has her work to do. Do you mind sitting here reading so that she can do her work?" She said, "I'll be glad to." So she sat there and she heard it all on May 18—the whole thing.

In the few short months that she worked with Bethune, Locklear was given more responsibility regarding her employer's financial affairs. Bethune wanted someone who would be able to work independently of her and be her right-hand assistant. On the last day of her life, she made a second request regarding her personal affairs.

And—I'm trying to think what things she did. Oh. When I came to work for her, I was just her personal secretary. She had two secretaries. I was her personal secretary, and Mrs. Bertha Mitchell was her business secretary for all of her financial affairs. And it was in April she said, "Senorita," she said, "You know I have been thinking, I don't see the need for having two secretaries. When I get ready for one thing, I have to ask you. When I get ready for another," she called her Loving, "I have to call her." Mrs. Loving, she was not there in the foundation. She was at the Bethune-Volusia Beach office. And she said, "And I have been watching you. Do you think that you could handle my business affairs, as well as my personal affairs?" I said, "I'll try." "I think you can do them both starting in May. I've watched you." So it started in May. So she got up and she called Mrs. Mitchell that day, and she said, "Loving, I've decided that I'm just gonna have Senorita to handle all of my affairs." So Mrs. Mitchell said, "That's fine, but I'll have to [get] the books up to date. So when I hand them to Senorita, I'm done." So she said, "Give me a couple weeks to bring it up to date." So after she did, she brought all of the ledgers up to the office. Mrs. Bethune said, "I want you to study these, and I want you to think of yourself as Mrs. Bethune, and when I ask you a question about my financial affairs, I expect you to answer it." So I said OK. On that day, she said, "Senorita, do you think that you are familiar enough with my affairs to handle it?" I said, "I think so." She said, "Well, good. It's all in your hands now."

The third thing was: "Oh, would you get the will out of the safe for me?" I got the will out, and she said, "I think I'll sign the will today." So I got it out of the safe, and she was going over it at her desk. She said, "Mmm, I'm getting a pain in my chest." So I said, "Well, maybe its indigestion." She said, "I don't know, but it's there." Well, I said, "Get up and walk; maybe you can walk it off." She got up from the desk, walked on the porch and sat. That's why I don't know why they—the rocking chair… that's the last place she sat before—and I don't know why they didn't keep the rocking chair. I've got several concerns that I have that disappeared. But she got up from the desk, she went on the porch and, sitting in the rocking chair, she was rocking, and I guess she had been out there ten or fifteen minutes. And Lucille came in (you know, Lucille was the niece who lived there). She called her "Mother Dear." She said, "Senorita, Mother Dear

*said move the papers off her desk. You know what she's talking about."
She didn't tell Lucille, she just told her to tell me to move the papers off of
her desk, and it was the will. Now that will had been in there for eleven
months and two—longer than that because it was there, and she had never
signed it. She had made changes. Oh, her will was old. She said, "I made
some changes." But that day, she said, "I want to look over it one more
time before I affix my signature." And that's what she had planned—to
sign it that day, but she started feeling bad and she got up. I got the will. I
put it back in the safe and locked it. She never signed it. So it was not in
effect. And when she left the bathroom, she went to the ladies' room on the
back porch (you know the little small toilet there) and that's where she was
stricken. When—well, I never leave the office. I could never leave the office
at five o'clock, you know how that is. I was always overtime. When I got
ready to leave, it was after six, and I went to the bathroom door. The door
was closed, and I knocked on the door. No, I didn't, I said, "Mrs. Bethune,
I'm leaving." She said, "Open the door." And I opened the door. She was
sitting on the stool, and this will forever ring in my ears. She said, "I'll see
you in the morning." I said OK—the last day.*

*And those three things that she did that day—and I believe she had a
premonition. There's no way, it's unusual…now, that will had been there
more than a year. She wanted to hear all of the chapters of her life at once,
and she wanted to know if I was familiar enough with her affairs to take over
as being her business and private secretary. But that day she had—well, she
had—I think she had…well, I'm just talking.*

There is very little audiovisual footage of Mary, but according to those
who knew her best, she had a very distinct walk that commanded attention.
She is often depicted as an older woman with a back issue and a cane, but
Locklear says that's inaccurate.

*And you talking bout somebody who could strut! If my back wasn't
hurting…you heard about her strut?*
No.
*Because now, before I retired, somebody over there, they did a skit on Mrs.
Bethune. And she came out with the cane, and that wasn't Mrs. Bethune.* [At
this point, Ms. Locklear stands up and demonstrates a walk with
a lady almost hunched over.] *Mrs. Bethune, she had the cane because you
know she needed it, but not like that. She didn't walk like that. Mrs. Bethune
would strut! Oh! I'm telling you!* [She demonstrates Mrs. Bethune's

walk with her head in the air.] *Her head high—tall! And I said, "Now, she didn't walk like that. Now she had a strut!" Two things: she was proud, she was determined and her eyes told a story.*

I'm trying to strut [laughs] *and my back is going…*

Although she'd accomplished much in her seventy-nine years of life, there were projects that Bethune was working on up until her last day. Her life was well spent, and she gave so much to many, but for her there was always a little more to give. When she started the Bethune Foundation, it was to be a place to share and inspire others with her vision, and over the years it continues to be such a place.

But I tell you, my concerns, one I didn't understand—oh, this is what I wanted to tell you in the part before. And she could write the most beautiful letters; they were full of so much wisdom, food for thought. You know what I told her one day? And this is what I was in the process of doing when she passed away. One day, she had just finished dictating a letter. You know, some people when you look at it, you can say, well, that's her, 'cause you know they have a pen phrase or something they can use in a letter and you can tell. Well, with Mrs. Bethune, every letter was different. So I told her one day, and she had just finished, I said, "Mrs. Bethune, have you ever thought about publishing your letters because there's too much wisdom in them for just the recipient to read." Everybody—you know what she said? "Would you like to do that?" And I was in the process of doing that when she passed away.

But when she passed away—see, the foundation was not a part of Bethune-Cookman; it was autonomous, the foundation was at that time. It was not Bethune, and Mrs. Bethune was the president, Mr. Davidson was the treasurer, but at any rate…I was called into the office, and they told me that Bethune-Cookman, their budget would not allow them to pay me to work. And that's how I got away because they had to take over the responsibility. See, Mrs. Bethune, she could raise that money. It was—and as I said, it was autonomous, but they said that they had to take over the foundation…the budget would not allow them, and they didn't have a secretary after that for a long, long time. So I came over, and I became secretary to Paul Hyde, who was the business manager at that time.

Oh yes. Another thing, you know that addition to the foundation?

Yes ma'am.

That brick part? Do you know what that was built for? To store her papers?

Yes, for research purposes. She wanted, for instance…it was gonna be a place to come to do research on her, and she had told Albert Bethune and me that she wanted us, when it was completed, to house everything and get it all set up. Now that was the reason she added that foundation—I mean that addition, that brick addition. She said, "I don't want it just to be a place for people to come in and look and see where I live." She said, "I want them to do their research right here." And that's what she built that room for, but she passed away before it was completed. So it didn't come to fruition—that didn't come to fruition.

Although Bethune didn't live to see the brick addition complete, it did happen, and today it is used as a space for student interns. Although it is not the research space she envisioned, it still provides opportunities for young minds to learn more about her life and to implement her ideals through their work in the home.

Part V

Galvanizing Women for Change Across the Sunshine State

Known as a "race woman" and deemed the "First Lady of Negro America," Mary McLeod Bethune was also very much an advocate for women's rights. She spent her early years building her school while also establishing herself as an invaluable leader in the clubwomen's movement. Rising to national prominence and starting her own women's organization, the National Council of Negro Women, in 1935, she always maintained a stake in local activism throughout the state of Florida, oftentimes bringing national attention to the state. Her closest allies in Florida—Eartha White and Ada Lee of Jacksonville—were leaders in their own communities but 100 percent behind Bethune in her efforts with B-CC and women's activism.

THE WOMEN'S ADVISORY BOARD

Throughout her lifetime, Bethune worked with many women's organizations, but the very first women's organization she founded was the Women's Advisory Board (WAB). Today, the WAB continues to support Bethune-Cookman University, and its work dates back to as early as 1911. After creating a trustee board of influential men, including playwright Harrison Garfield Rhodes, White Sewing Machine Company founder Thomas H. White and chemist and president of Proctor and Gamble

James N. Gamble, Bethune decided that a women's board to complement the trustees' fundraising was needed. Early members included Mrs. Ferris Meigs, Mrs. C.M. Ranslow, Miss Margaret Rhodes and Miss Jane Addams. Bethune invited Daytona's wealthiest women (many of whom were wives of the trustee board members) to work on the WAB to help fundraise and support the activities of the school. Many of the members had winter homes in Daytona Beach and actually lived in the North. The WAB was predominantly white in the earlier years, with the exception of Ladosia Adams (wife of Dr. Texas Adams) and Daisy Stockings (wife of Dr. John Stockings). Having prominent white members was a strategy that focused on attracting more white philanthropy by already having a show of visible support from influential whites. Attaching the school to influential names gave Bethune credibility, and it was also a networking tool. Over the years, more African Americans became members, including Alice Dunbar-Nelson (wife of poet Paul Laurence Dunbar), clubwoman and social worker Addie W. Dickerson and Bethune's dear friend and organizer of the Bethune Circle Mrs. Ada Lee.

The WAB was well known for its traditional annual bazaar (dating back to 1911), which brought in generous funds through the sale of baked goods, the school's farm-raised goods and various handmade items. For many years, the bazaar was held around the time of Valentine's Day and included dinner and a musical program. Vendors from the local community also joined the WAB and purchased tables to sell their goods. It is also noted that in the organization's early years, WAB members provided furniture for student rooms and for the infirmary. Although it was not a direct donation, members of the WAB arranged speaking opportunities with wealthy crowds for Bethune to discuss the work of the school. After she spoke to an integrated audience in 1927, the *Afro-American* newspaper wrote, "Her message had been tremendously inspiring and so human in its revelations of Mrs. Bethune's stern progress against great odds that many of the women who heard her gazed at her through tears." More times than not, she would captivate audiences and compel them to financially support her work. The WAB also hosted events to draw attention to the great work being done at the school, including an "At Home Day at the College." A key feature of the 1933 At Home Day at B-CC was the highlighting of the successful children's story hour held by the school librarian for the local community. Members felt that showing the success of the program, which attracted nearly three hundred children weekly, would help with solidifying more financial support. The WAB hosted cultural events on behalf of the school,

Mary and a member of the Women's Advisory Board speaking in White Hall on the campus of B-CC in 1949. *Courtesy of the Bethune-Cookman University Archives.*

and in 1953, members sponsored a concert in Daytona Beach featuring contralto and international superstar Marian Anderson. Anderson was a good friend of Bethune's and had worked with the National Council of Negro Women on various projects.

The WAB not only supported the school through fundraising, but the women were also very much invested in Mary's vision for the school. They attended commencement activities, encouraged fellow women to become involved in advancing the cause of the school and participated in the school's events. If it was not for the WAB, we might never have known Bethune-Cookman University as it is today. It is unclear why, but in 1919, the school made its third name change, transitioning from Daytona Educational and Industrial Institute to Daytona Normal and Industrial Institute. In 1923, the all-girls school began its merger with Cookman Institute and became known as Daytona Cookman Collegiate Institute. During a March 1925 meeting with the board of trustees, a WAB member recommended that the school name be changed to Bethune-Cookman College. The members felt that Bethune deserved to be recognized as the founder of the school, and the new name would reflect that. The women had established themselves as invaluable fundraisers, showing a total of over $2,000 in donations during the meeting. Because they'd established themselves as an asset to the trustee board, their voices were heard.

ADA LEE AND THE JACKSONVILLE BETHUNE CIRCLE

When Mrs. Bethune graduated from Moody Bible College in Chicago, she initially wanted to go to Africa to be a missionary but was told no, so she turned her attention to education. Lucy Craft Laney offered her her first teaching job at Haines Institute in Augusta, Georgia, in 1895. The pair developed a mentor/mentee relationship, and it was there that Bethune began to gather ideas for how she might one day start her own school. One of the ideas that Laney had established to assist the school with fundraising was Laney Leagues. Alumni and supporters of the school established the leagues in 1905 in the local community, and over the years, the program spread nationally. The leagues hosted fundraising events to support the efforts of Haines Institute. As Bethune struggled to raise money over the years, the creation of the Bethune Circle served a purpose similar to the leagues, providing critical funds for the school. The first Bethune Circle was founded in Jacksonville, Florida, in 1927 by one of Mary's closest friends, Ada M. Lee. She was also a member of B-CC's Women's Advisory Board. According to Dr. Sheila Flemming's text *The Answered Prayer to a Dream*, the Circle was led by the women of Ebenezer Methodist Church, including Isoline Whittington Vanderhorst, Eloise S. Lewey, Eloise Boyd, Mary Lewis, Thelma Ward, Ernestine Thompson, Anest Patterson Schell, Maggie Austin, Shelly Gibson and T.R. Sherman. Lee's husband, Ralph Lee, was the only man. Before merging with Bethune's all-girls school, Cookman Institute had maintained a presence in Jacksonville since 1872, so members of the community were very much connected to the newly established Bethune-Cookman College. In fact, Circle member Mrs. G.M. Scott was the wife of a former professor at Cookman Institute.

Founded for the purpose of the "uplift of humanity generally and the fostering of Bethune-Cookman College of Daytona Beach, Florida," the organization was structured with positions (president, second vice-president, secretary, assistant secretary and treasurer). Annual elections and voting processes were held for positions, and stockholders/directors meetings were held as well. The funds sent from the Circle were used for the immediate needs of the school, according to Bethune. In a 1938 letter she wrote to Lee, she told her friend that the $10.00 sent by Circle member Mrs. Rees was going to be used to paint the Domestic Science Department. A few months prior, after a concert sponsored by the Circle, Bethune had gratefully received $76.37, although it didn't specify what the funds would be used for. Although Lee was president, Bethune attended meetings and provided guidance for the direction of the Circle and called on her influential and wealthy Florida friends, including Jacksonville Federation leader Eartha M.M. White and Afro-American Life Insurance founder A.L. Lewis (who was also the state's first African American millionaire). She wrote asking him and his staff to support the Circle during a concert. She also encouraged Lee to reach out to old "Cookman-ites," Bethune-Cookman College Alumni in Jacksonville, Bishop R.A. Grant of the African Methodist Episcopal Church and the Second Baptist Church. For Bethune, the women of the Circle were grass-roots organizers who provided critical legwork for the school. Not only did they fundraise, but they also promoted the prominence of the school through community activities and functions. And she thanked them in her letters, filling them with thoughts of gratitude and words that conveyed how proud she was of them.

Lee took the lead in organizing engaging events to fundraise, particularly on holidays and special occasions that people usually celebrated. In 1935,

Ada M. Lee accepts the Mary McLeod Bethune Medallion in 1954. *Courtesy of the Bethune-Cookman University Archives.*

she arranged an "Easter Musical Festival" for the purpose of assisting with the purchase of furniture for the dining hall in B-CC's new building, Faith Hall (built in 1934). She often enlisted the help of local churches to host events. She held programs such as "Mary McLeod Bethune Night," in which she invited church choirs and local talent from around the city to perform solos and selections. Bethune would be the highlight of the programs as people came to see the NCNW president and presidential advisor. According to those who knew her best, she was a great orator, and her speeches were enjoyed by many.

During the 1930s, when the Great Depression threatened college enrollment, Lee led valiant efforts to bring more students into the school. She resigned as president in 1936, but by the next year, Bethune had nudged her back into the position. In a letter to Lee, she wrote:

> *We realize that you resigned from this position because of the pressure of business activities. However you are not now on the business roll, and our institution is greatly in need of your leadership in the splendid club that you organized nine years ago. Since the organization of the Circle, the Institution has received untold benefit from your activities. No member of our Advisory Board has been more arduous in her efforts to help lift the load, which confronts us. We want you to return to the "firing line," with your splendid group…to help us pull through the strategic year.*

At Bethune's urging, within a few months, Lee was again the president, and she would continue to serve the Circle until her 1956 passing shortly after she became president emeritus. In 1954, B-CC honored her with the Mary McLeod Bethune Medallion, which was given to outstanding individuals who embodied Bethune's spirit of leadership and dedication.

Over the years, the efforts of the Bethune Circle in Jacksonville laid the foundations for other B-CC supporters to organize chapters. The Bethune Circle #6 of New York was organized by Mrs. Pearl Cotton, and Mrs. Daisy Moore organized the Bethune Circle #7 of Newark, New Jersey. During the last year of Bethune's life, as she celebrated fifty years of B-CC, the two circles honored her with a celebration dinner and a gift of a $1,000 scholarship to the school. Faithful to the Circles, Mrs. Ada Lee attended the event along with Congressman Adam Clayton Powell, first African American principal in the east Mrs. Gertrude Ayer and Judge Thomas Dickens of New York City.

Clubwomen's Movement

After emancipation, African Americans faced new challenges in reestablishing womanhood and manhood. African American men attempted to establish patriarchal families in which they were the leaders. In some instances, men would relieve women from working outside the house to further establish themselves as heads of household, which made maintaining a household and raising the family priorities for women. However, with the onset of sharecropping and the necessity of female labor, the male's role as the sole provider was challenged, and the necessity of African American female labor challenged the stereotypical role of womanhood for less-privileged women. For African American women coming out of slavery, the turn of the twentieth century was focused on creating a positive image of womanhood. Many women asserted themselves in political matters to create positive images. In political arenas, women like Louisa and Lottie Rollins addressed the House of Representatives in 1869, expressing the need for universal suffrage. Black women also asserted themselves economically by successfully running large farms, sometimes alone, and proving that they could handle the double tasks of motherhood and work.

In Washington, D.C., on July 21, 1896, at the Nineteenth Street Baptist Church, the Colored Women's League (CWL) of Washington, D.C., and the National Federation of Afro-American Women (NFAAW) joined together to form the National Association of Colored Women's Clubs. The two women's organizations came together following a letter written by the president of the Missouri Press Association, James W. Jacks, in which he spoke of black women: "[They] were prostitutes and all were thieves and liars." The immorality of black women was a constant theme in speeches and publications. The periodical the *Independent* wrote that black women were said to have "brains of a child, the passions of a woman." In a 1902 edition of the periodical, one writer wrote that there was no way he could conceive a virtuous Negro woman. Fiction works such as *Three Lives*, written in 1909, also featured promiscuous African Americans, further advocating female immorality. Mary Jane Paterson, Mary Church Terrell and Anna Julia Cooper "called on a united black womanhood to solve the race's problems" and created CWL in 1892. NFAAW was founded in 1895 by St. Pierre Ruffin, and the first elected president was Margaret Murray Washington, wife of Booker T. Washington and dean of women at Tuskegee. Under the motto "Lifting As We Climb," NACW not only protested Jacks's letter but also set out to strengthen the image of black womanhood. The first president of NACW was Mary Church Terrell, a local Washingtonian born in Memphis, Tennessee; educated at Oberlin College; and active in politics and educational programing in D.C. Some of the key founders of the organization were anti-lynching activist and journalist Ida B. Wells, civil rights activist Josephine Silone Yates and abolitionist/poet Frances Harper.

As a self-help organization, NACW brought together hundreds of clubs from across the nation, including the Harriet Tubman Club of Boston; the Woman's Musical and Literary Club in Springfield, Missouri; the Semper Fidelis Club of Birmingham, Alabama; and Tuskegee Women's Clubs. Local clubs were led by state federations, which were all under the NACW. By 1914, the organization had nearly 100,000 members, and its departments included rescue work, mothers' meetings, kindergartens, professional businesswomen and temperance. As the national organization set the goals and mission of the organization, local chapters were responsible for implementing the objectives through action. Some of the objectives included eradicating illiteracy, supporting alcohol prohibition, ending the lynching of blacks and gaining full citizenship. *National Notes*, the organization's official publication, "served as an instrument to unite the women and to educate them in the sciences and techniques of reform."

On March 10, 1908, the Florida State Federation of Colored Women's Clubs was formed in St. Augustine under the leadership of Mrs. Harriet Dorrah. The following year, Bethune gave a speech at a national NACW meeting that wowed the organization, leaving Mary Church Terrell to predict that Bethune would someday be the organization's national president. As Bethune continued to grow her school in Daytona Beach, she became very active in the Florida clubwomen's movement. One of her closest friends and the head of the school's educational program, Frances Keyser, served as president of the Florida State Federation from 1912 to 1916. In 1916, Bethune was elected president, and she served until 1920. The Florida Federation consisted of various local clubs such as the Civil Improvement Club, the Sojourner Truth Club, the Amanda Smith Club, the Woman Development Club and the Women's Literary Art and Social Club. The organization worked with the mission to "better communities [and] lend a helping hand to the unfortunate girl." A focal point of Bethune's presidency was galvanizing federation members' support for American involvement in World War I. Under her leadership, the federation formed chapters of the Red Cross, purchased liberty bonds, preserved and canned food to reduce waste (making more food available for soldiers on frontlines) and taught people to live frugally by sewing/knitting their own clothing during the war. Women in city federations, including president of the Jacksonville City Federation Eartha M.M. White, worked hard to implement the statewide objectives.

Before the close of her term as president of the Florida State Federation, Bethune organized the Southeastern Federation of Colored Women's Clubs (SFCWC) to unify federations in Alabama, Arkansas, Florida, Georgia, Kentucky, Louisiana, Mississippi, Tennessee, North Carolina, South Carolina, West Virginia and Virginia. The organization was temporarily organized on January 16, 1920, in Daytona Beach, and during the NACW national convention at Tuskegee on July 12, 1920, SFCWC was formalized. Bethune was named as president. She brought together influential African American women from across the South, including principal and founder of Palmer Memorial Institute Mrs. Charlotte Hawkins Brown (vice-president), president and founder of St. Luke Penny Savings Bank Mrs. Maggie Lena Walker (chair of executive board) and educator Rebecca Stiles Taylor (corresponding secretary). The federation took on issues including reform in penal institutions, the abolition of Jim Crow cars, destruction of the "peonage system," the privilege to serve on juries and enforcement of the Fourteenth Amendment. A major accomplishment of the federation during Bethune's tenure was the purchase and operation of a delinquent girls' home in Ocala, Florida. She reached out to all African Americans across the state, including churches, secret societies and civic organizations, for assistance, and on September 25, 1921, the home was opened with the intent to reform troubled girls. In a 1923 letter from Bethune to the matrons of the home, she sent a personal check to assist with catching up the current expenses, stating, "Don't get discouraged [for] as long as I have a penny I am willing to share it with you. Don't give up. I am going to work and raise some money for you." To see the home succeed in reforming young lives and giving a second chance to girls who might not otherwise have been given one, she went to great lengths. In 1925, her tenure ended. As she toiled to keep the organizations she led alive, she also became an honorary member of Delta Sigma Theta sorority in 1923. Recognized for her leadership and excellence in the field of education, the organization bestowed on Bethune a membership just a decade after its historic founding.

After working her way up the local, state and regional ladder of the NACW, Mrs. Bethune became the eighth national president, serving from 1924 to 1928. She was preceded by Mary Church Terrell, Josephine Silone Yates, Lucy Thurman, Elizabeth Carter Brooks, Margaret Murray Washington, Mary B. Talbert and Hallie Q. Brown. By the time of her 1924 appointment as president of NACW, she had much experience working in and leading women's clubs. During the fifteenth biennial convention (in 1926), as president, Bethune announced plans to build a national headquarters by the next convention as a means to stabilize and centralize NACW's activities. During her address, she expressed ideals about the significance of the headquarters, stating, "We want unborn generations of Negro youth to map the national home of this federation a shrine to which they will make pilgrimages for inspiration. There will they find their ground for home in the carefully kept records and history of our people." At the end of Bethune's term as president in 1928, NACW's headquarters was purchased. During her 1926 address, she also expressed the importance staying abreast of the political and economic issues of colored people all over the world and called for a continued focus on both national and international issues. In the address, Bethune stated, "Bred, born and living here under the American flag, we nevertheless bear a relation to others of our blood. Their problems are ours and vice versa," encouraging members to take on the tasks of freedom and independence. Her speech also enlightened NACW to the commonality of the struggles of African Americans with other colored people of the world. Bethune's call for NACW to become concerned about the problems of others of the same blood outside America revealed a call of Pan-Africanist nature. Her interest was not only in studying the problems but also taking them on with dedication and vigor. During the convention, she announced a "Good Will and Inspection Tour" to Europe for the summer of 1927. She proposed that the trip would be one in which the organization would "observe and study" the industrial centers, caste problems, educational systems and governments of Europe. During the nine-country tour, Bethune and the women of NACW would meet Pope Pius XI, travel to poverty-stricken areas and meet various governing officials.

THE FOUNDING OF NATIONAL COUNCIL OF NEGRO WOMEN

The National Council of Negro Women (NCNW) was founded on December 5, 1935, at the 137th Street branch of the Young Women's Christian Association in New York City. Gathered together at a luncheon, thirty African American women from across the country came to take part in the possible inauguration of a new organization. Women such as Addie

Mary and the women of the National Council of Negro Women. *Courtesy of the Bethune-Cookman University Archives.*

Hunton, a national organizer for the National Association of Colored Women (NACW); Charlotte Hawkins Brown, founder and principal of Palmer Memorial Institute; Mabel Keaton Staupers, executive secretary of the National Association of Colored Graduate Nurses; and Daisy Lampkin, NAACP national secretary, attended the historic meeting. It was on this day that Mary would announce her desire to create a council of colored women that would serve as an umbrella organization to carry out collective missions under one voice.

After attending the 1927 National Council of Women meeting as a representative of NACW, Bethune was inspired to create the organization for black women. She wanted to end the exclusion of black women from the National Council of Women and other national organizations that barred or limited their participation. As she attended the White House Conference on Child Welfare, Bethune realized that "a super organization would have greater access to federal dispensation of funds." She also pushed forward with the idea of creating NCNW to bring unity among African American women's organizations in the public opinion and to create more cooperation as a whole among existing African American women's organizations. However, the organization was not created without some resistance. With women already heavily involved in the NAACP and other male-led organizations, and in light of the Great Depression, some felt that it was an inauspicious time to create an organization. The NACW was especially cold to Mary, as it felt that her organization would challenge its position as the leading black women's organization of its time. Mary Church Terrell was also particularly concerned that Bethune's organization would be useless. Although there were a few initial objections from women who did not understand the point of "another organization," a unanimous vote from the women at the meeting supported the idea. The women assembled at the meeting also pledged their support of her desire to create the National Council of Negro Women. Naturally, Bethune was voted to become the first president of the organization. During the first year of the NCNW, its business was conducted on the campus of Howard University, and Mary McLeod Bethune, Mary Church Terrell and Lucy D. Slowe were the directors.

In 1935, the United States was in the midst of an economic crisis known at the Great Depression. Although the United States was devastated by the effects of the Depression, African American communities were hit especially hard in the area of employment. Throughout various communities, the unemployment rates for African American women were sometimes four times that of their white counterparts. In 1935, the NAACP's legal battles for integration were expanding. NAACP lawyers Charles Houston and Thurgood Marshall fought a tough legal battle with the University of Maryland that resulted in Donald Murray becoming the first black student admitted to the University of Maryland Law School. Internationally, people of African descent rallied around Ethiopia as the Italians invaded one of only two African nations that remained untarnished by European colonialism. The lynching of African Americans had gained national attention, and in 1935, attempts were made to get President Franklin D. Roosevelt to support the Costigan-Wagner Anti-Lynching Bill. To the disappointment of African Americans all across the nation, the president refused to support the bill. For people of color, 1935 had been a year of ultimate highs and lows. But for Mary and the thirty women who joined her on December 5, 1935, it was a time to organize and unify to create change.

From its inception, the NCNW had a clear vision and purpose. One of the core principles of the organization was to bring unification to national organizations, particularly those that concerned African American women. Serving as an umbrella to over twenty-five organizations, the NCNW was able to implement calls to action in which each individual organization played a unique role. Many of the women who helped with the formation of the NCNW in 1935 were leaders in their communities, national civil rights organizations and the women's club movement. Developing leaders to continue the progression of the race educationally, economically and politically was at the core of NCNW's purpose.

Raising cultural awareness while also informing women on the issues concerning them was also at the center of the organization's mission. This commitment to inform was implemented through the founding of newsletters, journals and community events. Although the bulk of the NCNW's work was grounded in the United States, its purpose was to go beyond the domestic domain. The NCNW was committed to affiliating with international organizations as well. In the midst of building international relationships based solely on issues affecting women, the NCNW built cross-cultural bridges between women of color throughout the Caribbean and Africa.

The NCNW was strengthened not only by the organizations that joined as members but also by the women who led as president of the organization. From 1935 to 1949, Mary McLeod Bethune led the NCNW as its first president and founder. During her tenure, the organization became heavily involved in World War II efforts and sold $2 million in war bonds to raise the SS *Harriet Tubman*. This liberty ship was the first to honor an African American woman and was used to deliver vital supplies to troops stationed overseas during World War II. Under Bethune's leadership, the NCNW also became heavily involved in international affairs; often, the organization hosted local United Nations events. In 1940, the NCNW traveled to Cuba to host a women's conference with Cuba's leading feminist organization, the Asociación Cultural Femenina (Women's Cultural Association). A year later, the organization coordinated an annual conference in Haiti that was hosted by Elie Lescot, president of Haiti. During Bethune's tenure, she also established an international committee in 1946 to increase cultural awareness and to develop relationships internationally. One of Bethune's major accomplishments as president was establishing a national headquarters. In 1943, the NCNW purchased its national headquarters, located at 1318 Vermont Avenue in Washington, D.C., and from 1943 until 1966, all of the major meetings and events were hosted in there.

In the state of Florida, the NCNW took an active role in bringing Bethune's national ideas to the local level. Several sections made the trip to B-CC and the Mary McLeod Bethune Foundation to seek the guidance of the founder after her 1949 retirement. In March 1955, the Metropolitan section of St. Petersburg (Florida) was planning a pilgrimage to Daytona, where members would gather to hear Howard University instructor Dr. Margaret Just Butcher, theologian Howard Thurman, President Dr. Height and Bethune. They were to be hosted by the local Daytona Beach section. Less than two months later, Bethune passed away. A few years later, in 1961, Dorothy Height began a campaign to raise funds to erect a monument in honor of the founder in Washington, D.C. The Daytona Beach chapter spearheaded a local drive. In a 1961 letter in the *Daytona Morning Journal*, it encouraged the people of Daytona to contribute to the preservation of the memory of one of its finest citizens, and in 1974 the monument was erected. Today, NCNW continues to serve local communities throughout the nation because of Mrs. Bethune's unmatched leadership.

THE WOMEN'S ARMY CORP

During World War II (1939–45), when men were going off to war by the thousands, Representative Edith Nourse Rogers of Massachusetts introduced a bill to Congress to create the Women's Army Auxiliary Corp Act (WAAC) in May 1941. The act would create voluntary, noncombat positions such as clerical workers, cooks, phone operators and medical-related jobs. After the December 7, 1941 attack on Pearl Harbor, the United States became fully immersed in the war. Creation of the WAAC would allow more men to be on the frontline and free from noncombat positions. One year later, on May 14, 1942, the act became a bill, and the following day, President Franklin D. Roosevelt signed it into law, making Oveta Culp Hobby the first director. Due to the promotion of John Thompson's call for "Double Victory" throughout African American newspapers and media, African Americans also became involved in the war on the frontlines as soldiers and took on defense-related jobs. The Double Victory called for African Americans to join war efforts to fight against fascism for victory abroad and against discrimination and racism for victory at home. Although the campaign caught on, there were some who were skeptical about how the war would actually help African Americans, among them W.E.B. Dubois. In a speech to the local Chicago community, he stated, "The popular notion that World War II was a fight to the finish between democracy and fascism is false." Bethune, however, did not side with Dubois and promoted the war through the NCNW as an advocate for women's involvement.

Behind the scenes, it was Bethune who fought for the inclusion of African American women as WAAC members. In her 2011 memoir, *Justice Older Than the Law*, former WAAC officer Dovey Johnson Roundtree recalled watching Mary meet with First Lady Roosevelt in attempts to get "her girls" involved in the war. The first lady was leery about having African American women serve alongside white women, but Bethune did not back down. Roundtree wrote, "Watching Dr. Bethune fight so hard over so many months for a place for black women in the military, I came to the conclusion that for all my reservations and fears, I couldn't turn away from her challenge." It was due to Bethune's continued persistence that the first class of officers for the WAAC began their July 1942 training in Des Moines, Iowa, and approximately thirty-nine African American female officers were among that number. Approximately 10.6 percent of the WAAC's members were to be African American women, and in its early phase, Bethune saw to it that that number was fulfilled.

Mrs. Bethune became a special assistant to Secretary of War Harry L. Stimson and was responsible for handpicking the first forty members of WAAC. In choosing the members, she picked women who were college educated and whom she felt would best represent their race. She went throughout the United States recruiting on college campuses to find women to serve. On the first day of training, she met the women in Des Moines and checked out the facilities to ensure that the women were in livable conditions. Remembering the sobering effect of Bethune's visit, Dovey Roundtree wrote, "She gathered her girls about her…and reminded us of our place in history." She also wrote, "Dr. Bethune transformed the atmosphere of those uneasy hours with a few carefully chosen words." She didn't just throw the women into action; she paid a personal visit to ensure their safety and to give them a boost of confidence. Over the years, she would be a supporter of the women and a confidante they could trust. After being personally selected by Bethune, Roundtree went on to become a lieutenant in the corps, eventually leading her to Daytona Beach. In 1943, she recruited three young women from Bethune's city: Johny B. Chambers, from the community of Pine Haven; Mae Hart of Daytona; and B-CC student Dorothy B. Shepard. The joining of three of Daytona Beach's own, particularly one who was a student, was a proud moment for Bethune.

Understanding both the critical need for women's participation to win the war and the positive economic possibilities presented by the war, Bethune sought yet another opportunity, particularly for Daytona Beach. The first training site for WAACs opened in Des Moines, Iowa, but in that same year, a second site opened in Daytona Beach, largely due to Bethune's lobbying efforts. The war had a negative impact on the economy of the tourist town of Daytona Beach, and she felt that having a training site would improve it. She was right. In October 1942, the first WAACs arrived, living out of tents and, later, beachside motels. In an interview with former WAAC member Mildred C. Bailey, she talked about her arrival in Daytona Beach:

> We started out taking over the hotels. The hotels were boarded up. That's all in my book. The hotels were all boarded up because there were no tourists, no gas. We took over the hotels and moved our troops into them, used the ballparks for parade grounds. The hotels that were on the beach, when the tide was out, we went down and learned to march. By the end of the year, this was a very, very difficult situation, and no transportation of any kind. They decided to build temporary billets away from the beach. They were in the middle of building that when I left, had taken over the command of a company. All that conversation you're going to listen to, it tells about everything that happened there. I stayed there about eighteen months, I think.

The arrival of the base quickly changed the economy of Daytona Beach for the good and provided almost $5 million in monthly revenue. Although Bethune's fight for inclusion of African American women succeeded in gaining the first thirty-nine women in Des Moines, the same opportunities were not offered in Daytona. On December 12, 1942, the *Chicago Defender* ran an article titled "'Whites Only' at Daytona Beach WAAC Camp," revealing that there were facilities in the city, but none was open to training African American women. The War Department issued the following statement, "Negro units will not be available for the Second Women's Army Auxiliary Corp Training Center opening at Daytona Beach, Fla. December 1," which didn't fully rule out the possibility of later opening them to African Americans.

Despite these issues, Bethune continued to support the efforts of the war. She began to use her influential role as president of the NCNW to draw concern to the general welfare of soldiers abroad and pushed for the organization to be on the advisory council on soldiers' welfare. In a letter to Stimson published in the *Atlanta Daily World*, she advised the general, "We still seek this end and urge upon you that Negro representation be included in this advisory until and in all future plans." In her protest, she also reiterated the connection between the inclusion of African Americans and democracy. She often told the government that African Americans receiving equal treatment and equal opportunities were a vital extension of American democracy. By 1943, the NCNW was represented by Dorothy Porter, as a member of the Advisory Council for the Women's Interests Section. The organization was formed to inform women about the welfare of soldiers and distributed information about soldiers' health, available recreational activities and how women could contribute to the war. With Bethune and the NCNW's involvement, they were inserted into every aspect of the war.

The first thirty-nine African American women to go into the WAAC were the first women to serve in the military other than nurses. Prior to their arrival, all of the military members had been men. For the women, it was a scary yet historic time. In Dovey Roundtree's text, she recalled explaining her desire to enlist in the WAAC despite her grandmother and mother, who "regarded the military with fear." The WAAC's members and their families did not know what to expect. As a recruiter and advisor, Bethune utilized her organization to calm the fears of African Americans. In the 1942 anniversary pre-conference issue of *Aframerican Women's Journal*, the NCNW featured the WAAC in the article "The W.A.A.C.—The Girl Who Wouldn't Be Left Behind." The journal emphasized the historical significance of the WAAC, featured information about Director Oveta Culp Hobby and provided an outline of the typical daily requirements of a WAAC member. The article also featured the names and contact information for the women who graduated from the officer's training school. The journal updated the community on the conditions of the women of the WAAC.

The Last Words of a Legendary Woman

As life drew to a close, Mary McLeod Bethune desired to leave a gift to the world through the writing of her last will and testament. Published in the August 1955 subscription of *Ebony* magazine, throughout the essay Bethune left her insight and philosophies for generations to come so that they, too, might make a valuable contribution to the world as she did. As a woman who started life as the daughter of formerly enslaved parents in rural South Carolina, she knew the challenges that one could face when trying to create change. Setbacks were familiar to Bethune, but she mastered how to turn them into success. Over the years, as she rose to become an influential voice in America and beyond, she maintained a special connection with Florida and made it her home. For Bethune, the state was the place where she'd begun a journey in taking a stance against educational equality with the founding of her school 1904 and the place where she stood for justice for all as a leader in the clubwoman's movement. By the end of her career, many knew her for her national and international activism, but Florida was the place where she developed invaluable leadership skills in the earlier years.

Today, Mary McLeod Bethune's name continues to resonate throughout the Sunshine State, as Bethune-Cookman University still stands in Daytona Beach, Bethune Beach continues to be a place of residence for many and the Mary McLeod Bethune Foundation welcomes visitors from all walks of life into her home. The work of creating political change continues as organizations, including the National Council of Negro Women, Women's Advisory Board, National Association of Colored Women and Delta Sigma

Theta Sorority Inc., continue to serve their local communities in Florida and, for some, throughout the nation. Although she has departed, the legacy of Mrs. Mary McLeod Bethune continues on.

Mary McLeod Bethune
MY LAST WILL AND TESTAMENT...
SOMETIMES as I sit communing in my study I feel that death is not far off. I am aware that it will overtake me before the greatest of my dreams—full equality for the Negro in our time—is realized. Yet, I face that reality without tears or regrets. I am resigned to death, as all humans must be at the proper time. Death neither alarms nor frightens one who has a long career of fruitful toil. The knowledge that my work has been helpful to many fills me with joy and great satisfaction.

Since my retirement from an active role in educational work and from the affairs of the National Council of Negro Women, I have been living quietly and working at my desk at my home here in Florida. The years have directed a change of pace for me. I am now 78 years old and my activities are no longer so strenuous as they once were. I feel that I must conserve my strength to finish the work at hand.

Already I have begun working on my autobiography which will record my life-journey in detail, together with the innumerable side trips which have carried me abroad, into every corner of our country, into homes both lowly and luxurious, and even into the White House to confer with Presidents. I have also deeded my home and its contents to the Mary McLeod Bethune Foundation, organized in March 1953, for research, interracial activity and the sponsorship of wider educational opportunities.

Sometimes I ask myself if I have any other legacy to leave. Truly, my worldly possessions are few. Yet, my experiences have been rich. From them, I have distilled principles and policies in which I believe firmly, for they represent the meaning of my life's work. They are the product of much sweat and sorrow. Perhaps in them there is something of value. So, as my life draws to a close, I will pass them on to Negroes everywhere in the hope that an old woman's philosophy may give them inspiration.

Here, then is my legacy.

I leave you love. Love builds. It is positive and helpful. It is more beneficial than hate. Injuries quickly forgotten quickly pass away. Personally and racially, our enemies must be forgiven. Our aim must be to create a world of fellowship and justice where no man's skin, color or religion, is held against him. "Love thy neighbor" is a precept which could transform the world if it were universally practiced. It connotes brotherhood and, to me, brotherhood of man is the noblest concept in all human relations. Loving your neighbor means being interracial, interreligious and international.

I leave you hope. The Negro's growth will be great in the years to come. Yesterday, our ancestors endured the degradation of slavery, yet they retained their dignity. Today, we direct our economic and political strength toward winning a more abundant and secure life. Tomorrow, a new Negro, unhindered by race taboos and shackles, will benefit from more than 330 years of ceaseless striving and struggle. Theirs will be a better world. This I believe with all my heart.

I leave you the challenge of developing confidence in one another. As long as Negroes are hemmed into racial blocs by prejudice and pressure, it will be

MARY McLEOD BETHUNE
1875 - 1955

Funeral Services

Monday Afternoon, May Twenty-Third
Nineteen Hundred Fifty-Five
Two O'clock

Bethune-Cookman College Auditorium
Daytona Beach, Florida

The 1955 funeral program for Mary McLeod Bethune. *Courtesy of the Bethune-Cookman University Archives.*

necessary for them to band together for economic betterment. Negro banks, insurance companies and other businesses are examples of successful racial economic enterprises. These institutions were made possible by vision and mutual aid. Confidence was vital in getting them started and keeping them going. Negroes have got to demonstrate still more confidence in each other in business. This kind of confidence will aid the economic rise of the race by bringing together the pennies and dollars of our people and ploughing them into useful channels. Economic separatism cannot be tolerated in this enlightened age, and it is not practicable. We must spread out as far and as fast as we can, but we must also help each other as we go.

I leave you a thirst for education. Knowledge is the prime need of the hour. More and more, Negroes are taking full advantage of hard-won opportunities for learning, and the educational level of the Negro population is at its highest point in history. We are making greater use of the privileges inherent in living in a democracy. If we continue in this trend, we will be able to rear increasing numbers of strong, purposeful men and women, equipped with vision, mental clarity, health and education.

I leave you a respect for the uses of power. We live in a world which respects powers above all things. Power, intelligently directed, can lead to more freedom. Unwisely directed, it can be a dreadful, destructive force. During my lifetime I have seen the power of the Negro grow enormously. It has always been my first concern that this power should be placed on the side of human justice. Now that the barriers are crumbling everywhere, the Negro in America must be ever vigilant less his forces be marshaled behind wrong causes and undemocratic movements. He must not lend his support to any group that seeks to subvert democracy. That is why we must select leaders who are wise, courageous, and of great moral stature and ability. We have great leaders among us today: Ralph Bunche, Channing Tobias, Mordecai Johnson, Walter White, and Mary Church Terrell. [All of these leaders are now deceased.] *We have had other great men and women in the past: Frederick Douglass, Booker T. Washington, Harriet Tubman, Sojourner Truth. We must produce more qualified people like them who will work not for themselves, but for others.*

I leave you faith. Faith is the first factor in a life devoted to service. Without faith, nothing is possible. With it, nothing is impossible. Faith in God is the greatest power, but great, too, is faith in oneself. In 50 years the faith of the American Negro in himself has grown immensely and is still increasing. The measure of our progress as a race is in precise relation to the depth of the faith in our people held by our leaders. Frederick Douglass, genius though he was, was spurred by a deep conviction that his people would heed his counsel and follow him to freedom. Our greatest Negro figures have been imbued with faith. Our forefathers struggled for liberty in conditions far more onerous than those we now face, but they never lost the faith. Their perseverance paid rich dividends. We must never forget their sufferings and their sacrifices, for they were the foundations of the progress of our people.

I leave you racial dignity. I want Negroes to maintain their human dignity at all costs. We, as Negroes, must recognize that we are the custodians as well as the heirs of a great civilization. We have given something to the world as a race and for this we are proud and fully conscious of our place in the total picture of mankind's development. We must learn also to share and mix with all men. We must make an effort to be less race conscious and more conscious of individual and human values. I have never been sensitive about my complexion. My color has never destroyed my self-respect nor has it ever caused me to conduct myself in such a manner as to merit the disrespect of any person. I have not let my color handicap me. Despite many crushing burdens and handicaps, I have risen from the cotton fields of South Carolina to found a college, administer it during its years of growth, become a public servant in the government of our country and leader of women. I would not exchange my color for all the wealth in the world, for had I been born white I might not have been able to do all that I have done or yet hope to do.

I leave you a desire to live harmoniously with your fellow men. The problem of color is worldwide. It is found in Africa and Asia, Europe and South America. I appeal to American Negroes—North, South, East and West—to recognize their common problems and unite to solve them. I pray that we will learn to live harmoniously with the white race. So often, our difficulties have made us hypersensitive and truculent. I want to see my people conduct themselves naturally in all relationships—fully conscious of their manly responsibilities and deeply aware of their heritage. I want them to learn to understand whites and influence them for good, for it is advisable and sensible for us to do. We are a minority of 15 million living side by side with a white majority. We must learn to deal with these people positively and on an individual basis.

I leave you finally a responsibility to our young people. The world around us really belongs to youth for youth will take over its future management. Our children must never lose their zeal for building a better world. They

The last known photo of Mrs. Bethune, taken in April 1955.

must not be discouraged from aspiring toward greatness, for they are to be the leaders of tomorrow. Nor must they forget that the masses of our people are still underprivileged, ill-housed, impoverished and victimized by discrimination. We have a powerful potential in our youth, and we must have the courage to change old ideas and practices so that we may direct their power toward good ends.

Faith, courage, brotherhood, dignity, ambition, responsibility—these are needed today as never before. We must cultivate them and use them as tools for our task of completing the establishment of equality for the Negro. We must sharpen these tools in the struggle that faces us and find new ways of using them. The Freedom Gates are half-a-jar. We must pry them fully open.

If I have a legacy to leave my people, it is my philosophy of living and serving. As I face tomorrow, I am content, for I think I have spent my life well. I pray now that my philosophy may be helpful to those who share my vision of world Peace, Progress, Brotherhood and Love.

Bibliography

PART I

Allen, Cleveland G. "Education of Race in South Neglected, Says Dr. Mary M. Bethune." *Chicago Defender*, July 3, 1937.

Bethune, Mary McLeod. "Have No Fear for the New Year; 'Tomorrow Will Be Brighter.'" *Chicago Defender*, January 8, 1949.

———. Interview with Dr. Charles Johnson, 1940. Florida Memory Project. https://www.floridamemory.com/onlineclassroom/marybethune/lessonplans/sets/interview.

Chicago Defender. "Fla. Students in Interracial Discussion: Mrs. Bethune Welcomes Delegates to Bethune-Cookman College." March 11, 1939.

———. "Negro College Fund Now Totals $901,812." November 27, 1944.

Dickinson, Joy Wallace. "Passion for Learning Put a Legend on Path to Greatness." *Orlando Sentinel*, May 2, 2004.

Durr, Virginia Foster. Southern Oral History Program interview with Virginia Foster Durr, October 16, 1975. Southern Oral History Program Collection. Southern Historical Collection, Wilson Library, University of North Carolina–Chapel Hill.

———. Southern Oral History Program interviews with Virginia Foster Durr, March 13, 14 and 15, 1975. Southern Oral History Program Collection. Southern Historical Collection, Wilson Library, University of North Carolina–Chapel Hill.

Flemming, Sheila Y. *Bethune-Cookman College, 1904–1994: The Answered Prayer to a Dream*. Virginia Beach, VA: Donning Company Publishers, 1995.

Gasman, Marybeth. *Envisioning Black Colleges: A History of the United Negro College Fund*. Baltimore, MD: Johns Hopkins University Press, 2007.

Holt, Rackham. *Mary McLeod Bethune: A Biography*. New York: Doubleday & Company, 1964.

Bibliography

Jackson, David H. "Tour of the Sunshine State, March 1912." In *Booker T. Washington and the Struggle Against White Supremacy: The Southern Educational Tours, 1908–1912.* New York: Palgrave Macmillian, 2008.

Literary Digest. "Negro Angel: Mary McLeod Bethune, College Founder, Sees Bright Future for Her Race." March 6, 1937.

Lucas, Harold V., Jr. Interview by Ashley Robertson. Daytona Beach, December 8, 2014.

New York Amsterdam News. "Mrs. Bethune Did It." March 9, 1940.

Ortiz, Paul. *Emancipation Betrayed: The Hidden History of Black Organizing and White Violence in Florida from Reconstruction to the Bloody Election of 1920.* Berkeley: University of California Press, 2005.

Pickens, William. "The Story of Mary McLeod Bethune Bares South's Educational 'Equality.'" *Chicago Defender,* November 26, 1921.

Seymour, Mary. "The Ghosts of Rollins." *Rollins Magazine* (Fall 2011).

Smith, Elaine M., and Audrey Thomas McCluskey, eds. *Mary McLeod Bethune: Building a Better World.* Bloomington: Indiana University Press, 1999.

PART II

Adams, Cal. "Mrs. Bethune to Devote Rest of Her Life to Work on New Educational Foundation." *St. Petersburg Times,* June 14, 1953.

"Annual Financial Statements." Mary McLeod Bethune Foundation Papers. Mary McLeod Bethune Foundation #1 Folder. Mary McLeod Bethune Foundation National Historic Landmark, Bethune-Cookman University, Daytona Beach, FL.

"Annual Report of the President." Mary McLeod Bethune Foundation Papers. Mary McLeod Bethune Foundation #1 Folder. Mary McLeod Bethune Foundation National Historic Landmark, Bethune-Cookman University, Daytona Beach, FL.

Bethune, Mary McLeod. "The Mary McLeod Bethune Foundation Has Been Born to Inspire Posterity." *Chicago Defender,* April 11, 1953.

Chicago Defender. "Mrs. Bethune Fights Race Ban at Daytona Beach Auditorium." October 15, 1949.

Green, Jada Wright. "Honoring Her Legacy." *Legendary Retreat Newsletter* (Spring 2014). http://issuu.com/bethunesretreat (accessed December 20, 2014).

Miami News. "Dr. Bethune Gives Home to Foundation." March 18, 1953.

National Park Service. "National Historic Landmarks Program." Overview of the Nomination Process. http://www.nps.gov/nhl/apply/intro.htm (accessed December 28, 2014).

———. "National Register of Historic Places." National Register of Historic Places Official Website. www.nps.gov/nr (accessed December 28, 2014).

Pettus, Patricia. "Retreat Memories: Wonderful Times Shared with Mother Dear." *Legendary Retreat Newsletter* (Winter 2013–14): 3. http://issuu.com/bethunesretreat (accessed December 18, 2014).

Smith, Elaine M., and Audrey Thomas McCluskey, eds. *Mary McLeod Bethune: Building a Better World.* Bloomington: Indiana University Press, 1999.

St. Petersburg Times. "Local Woman at Dedication of Foundation." March 24, 1953.

Bibliography

PART III

Bethune, Albert McLeod, Jr. Interview by Ashley Robertson. Daytona Beach, November 25, 2014.

Bethune, Mary McLeod. "Last Will and Testament." *Ebony*, August 1955.

———. "Let's Help Save the Bethune Beach Project." *Memphis World*, July 25, 1952.

———. "Mary McLeod Bethune Writes." *Chicago Defender*, April 4, 1936.

———. "Thousands Flock to Bethune-Volusia Beach; Answer to a 34-Year Dream." *Chicago Defender*, August 2, 1952.

Catron, Derek. "Blacks Recall Segregation in Daytona." *Orlando Sentinel*, July 12, 1998. http://articles.orlandosentinel.com/1998-07-12/news/9807120309_1_black-college-reunion-daytona-beach-famous-beach.

Daily Journal, April 16, 1993. George Engram Collection, Bethune-Cookman University Archives, Daytona Beach, FL.

Florida Crossroads. *Paradise Lost: Florida's Segregated Beaches*. Online video. Florida Channel, 2014.

Grimison, Matt. "Historically Black Beach Fades into Memory After Integration." *Orlando Sentinel*, October 13, 2003. http://articles.sun-sentinel.com/2003-10-13/news/0310120463_1_bethune-beach-bethune-volusia-beach-real-estate.

Laird, Susan. "American Beach Fights to Preserve a Place in History." *Ocala Star-Banner*, January 21, 1995.

Lempel, Leonard R. "The Origins of the Civil Rights Movement in Daytona Beach." Faculty research, Bethune-Cookman University.

Memphis World. "African Students' Union Convenes in Daytona Beach." January 1, 1950.

———. "Bethune Beach Host to Motorcycle Races April 5." March 27, 1953.

———. "Over 500 Home Sites Sold at Bethune Beach." February 2, 1951.

———. "Over 5,000 at Bethune Beach, Fla., July 4." July 11, 1950.

Powell, Mary Alice. "St. Augustine Treasures Its African-American History." *The Blade*, February 15, 2004.

Report of Board of Directors, December 9, 1945. J.N. Crooms Collection, Series 3, Box 3, Folder 1.2. John G. Riley Archives, Tallahassee Community College, Tallahassee, FL.

Rizzo, Marian. "Paradise Park Was a Haven for Black Community." *Ocala Star-Banner*, August 22, 2013.

Schmich, Mary T. "They Had a Dream: Bethune Beach." *Orlando Sentinel*, March 31, 1985.

Scott, Mrs. W.A., Sr. "Gathered Here and There: Bethune Volusia Beach." *Memphis World*, July 18, 1952.

PART IV

Bethune, Albert McLeod, Jr. Interview by Ashley Robertson. Daytona Beach, January 8, 2015.

Higgins, Cleo Mcray. Interview by Ashley Robertson. Daytona Beach, January 6, 2015.

Bibliography

Locklear, Senorita. W. Interview by Ashley Robertson. Daytona Beach, December 10, 2014.

Lucas, Harold V., Jr. Interview by Ashley Robertson. Daytona Beach, December 8, 2014.

Part V

Afro American-Baltimore. "Banquet for Dr. Bethune." April 6, 1954.

————. "Jane Addams Lauds Mary Bethune." April 23, 1927.

Bailey, Mildred C. Interview, May 26, 1999. Betty H. Carter Women Veterans Historical Project. Mildred Caroon Bailey Papers, UNCG Digital Collections, University of North Carolina–Greensboro. Available online at http://libcdm1.uncg.edu/cdm.

Bethune, Mary McLeod. "In Token of a Common Humanity We Must Give Grain to India(2)." *Chicago Defender*, April 28, 1951.

————. "Mrs. Bethune Gives an Inspiring Word or Two to the People of Nassau." *Chicago Defender*, May 9, 1953.

————. "The People, the Land, the Economy of a Revelation—Bethune." *Chicago Defender*, August 6, 1949.

————. "We Need Love—Mrs. Bethune." *Afro American*, November 25, 1950.

"Bethune Serving as President, Southeastern Federation of Colored Women's Clubs, 1923." Eartha White Collection, Mary McLeod Bethune Papers, 1919–1955. Folder G. Thomas G. Carpenter Library Archives, University of North Florida, Jacksonville, FL.

Bracey, John H., Jr., and August Meir. *Records of the National Association of Colored Women's Clubs, 1895–1992*. Part 1. Bethesda, MD: University Publications of America, 1994.

Central Florida Memory Digital Archives. "The B-Cean, 1954." Digital Services Unit of the University of Central Florida Libraries.

————. "Bethune-Cookman College: *The Advocate* 46, 1951–1952." Digital Services Unit of the University of Central Florida Libraries.

————. "Bethune Cookman University: *The Wildcat*, 1930." Digital Services Unit of the University of Central Florida Libraries.

————. "Bethune/Grillo Family Photograph." Bethune Cookman University Photograph Collection, Digital Services Unit of the University of Central Florida Libraries.

Chicago Defender. "Daytona-Cookman Collegiate Institute." March 27, 1926.

————. "'No Fight Against Fascism in World War II'—DuBois." June 8, 1946.

————. "3 Daytona Beach Girls Join WAACs." May 8, 1943.

Collier-Thomas, Bettye. *Jesus Jobs and Justice: African American Women and Religion*. New York: Alfred A. Knopf, 2010.

"Committee on By-laws and Constitution Report, May 3, 1934." Bethune Clubs: Bethune Circle of Jacksonville Papers. Bethune-Cookman University Archives, Daytona Beach, FL.

Daytona Beach Morning Journal. "Bahamas Leader Arrives." March 16, 1970.

———. "Dr. Bethune Brings Frisco Confab Story to Daytona Beach." June 9, 1945.

———. "Great Negro Contralto to Sing Tonight." Friday, March 20, 1953.

———. "Vet Businessmen Hear College President." October 27, 1948.

Daytona Beach Sunday News-Journal. "Clubs: Silver Leaf." February 5, 1956.

"Edith Nourse Rogers: Representative, 1925–1960, Republican from Massachusetts." Women in Congress. http://womenincongress.house.gov/member-profiles/profile.html?intID=209.

Eisenhower, Dwight D. "Letter to Secretary Dulles Regarding Transfer of the Affairs of the Foreign Operations Administration to the Department of State." April 17, 1955. Gerhard Peters and John T. Woolley, the American Presidency Project.

Florida Star. "Famed Bethune-Cookman College Ensemble to Sing Here." March 3, 1956. George A. Smathers Libraries, University of Florida Digital Collections. http://ufdc.ufl.edu/UF00028362/00262/5x?search=bethune&vo=02.

Giddings, Paula J. *When and Where I Enter: The Impact of Black Women on Race and Sex in America*. New York: William Morrow Paperbacks, 1996.

Grillo, Evelio. *Black Cuban, Black American: A Memoir*. Houston, TX: Arte Publico Press, 2000.

Guridy, Frank Andre. *Forging Diaspora: Afro-Cubans and African Americans in a World of Empire and Jim Crow*. Chapel Hill: University of North Carolina, 2010.

Hobby, Colonel Oveta Culp. "WAACs at Work." *Chicago Defender*, September 26, 1942.

Jones, Ida. *Mary McLeod Bethune in Washington, D.C.* Charleston, SC: The History Press, 2013.

Leslie, LaVonne. *The History of the National Association of Colored Women's Clubs, Inc.* N.p.: Xlibris Corporation, 2012.

Letter from Lamar Fort to Bethune, June 10, 1947. Part 2, Reel 4. Mary McLeod Bethune Foundation Papers. Bethune-Cookman University Archives, Daytona Beach, FL.

Light, Patti. *Daytona Beach Lifeguards*. Charleston, SC: Arcadia Publishing, 2010.

"Mary McLeod Bethune Night Program." Eartha White Collection, Mary McLeod Bethune Papers, 1919–1955. Folder G. Thomas G. Carpenter Library Archives, University of North Florida, Jacksonville, FL.

"Mary McLeod Bethune to Ada Lee, October 11, 1937." Bethune Clubs: Bethune Circle of Jacksonville Papers. Bethune-Cookman University Archives, Daytona Beach, FL.

McAlpin, Harry. "Whites Only at Daytona Beach WAAC Camp." *Chicago Defender*, December 12, 1942.

McCabe, Katie, and Dovey Johnson Roundtree. *Justice Older Than the Law: The Life of Dovey Johnson Roundtree*. Jackson: University Press of Mississippi, 2009.

McCluskey, Audrey Thomas. *A Forgotten Sisterhood: Pioneering Black Women Educators and Activists in the Jim Crow South*. Lanham, MD: Rowman & Littlefield, 2014.

McComb, Mary C. *Great Depression and the Middle Class: Ideology, 1929–1941*. New York: Routledge, 2006.

National Association for the Advancement of Colored People Press Release, May 8, 1945. W.E.B. DuBois Papers (MS 312). Special Collections and University Archives.

Bibliography

"Notes on the Florida State Federation." Part 1, Reel 6, Slides 456–458. Records of the National Association for Colored Women. Bethune-Cookman University Archives, Daytona Beach, FL.

"Report of President Bethune, to Advisory Board, December 14, 1932." Board of Trustees/Women's Advisory Board Papers. Bethune-Cookman University Archives, Daytona Beach, FL.

Smith, Elaine M., and Audrey Thomas McCluskey, eds. *Mary McLeod Bethune: Building a Better World.* Bloomington: Indiana University Press, 1999.

St. Petersburg Times. "Liberian Farm Expert Coming Home on Visit." November 28, 1956.

White, Deborah Gray. *Too Heavy a Load: Black Women in Defense of Themselves, 1894–1994.* New York: W.W. Norton & Company, 1999.

White, Walter. "People, Politics and Places." *Chicago Defender,* May 19, 1945.

CONCLUSION

Bethune, Mary McLeod. "Last Will and Testament." *Ebony* (August 1955).

Index

Index

U

United Nations 43, 44, 46, 47, 123
United Negro College Fund 36, 135

W

Washington, Booker T. 18, 34, 41, 117,
        132, 136
Washington, Margaret Murray 18,
        117, 119
Welricha Motel 74, 75, 77
Westside Business and Professional
        Men's Association 53
White, Eartha M.M. 115, 119
White, Thomas 18, 31, 53, 54
White, Walter 43, 44, 132
Women's Advisory Board 111, 114, 140
Women's Army Auxiliary Corp 124, 126
World War II 24, 37, 123, 124, 138

Z

Zeiger, Carol Robin 56

About the Author

Ashley N. Robertson, PhD, was born in Oxford, North Carolina, and is a curator and museum director for the Mary McLeod Bethune Foundation/ National Historic Landmark at Bethune-Cookman University, where she is also an assistant professor of history. Dr. Robertson graduated from Howard University in 2013 with a PhD in African Diaspora history, and she also holds a bachelor's degree in business administration from Bowie State University and a master of arts in African American studies from Temple University. She has been inspired by the legacy and life of her (s)hero, Mary McLeod Bethune, and she truly believes in her words: "Knowledge is the prime need of the hour."